Home Remedies

Home Remedies

ALTERNATIVE · THERAPIES ·

Betty Kirkpatrick

LUCEM · LIBRIS
DISSEMINAMUS

**GEDDES&
GROSSET**

This edition published 2007 by Geddes & Grosset

© 1996 Geddes & Grosset
David Dale House, New Lanark ML11 9DJ, Scotland

First edition published 1996
Reprinted 1999, 2007

ISBN 978 1 85534 219 4

Printed and bound in India

Introduction

Nowadays when there is anything wrong with us we are used to purchasing a whole range of patent medicines over the pharmacist's counter or to going to our GP to get a drug especially prescribed for us. This, however, is a recent development in the history of mankind. The drugs revolution did not really get under way until after World War II, although of course doctors had recourse to a range of medications before that.

In contrast with the drugs revolution, folk medicine dated back into the mists of time. There is archaeological evidence that primitive human beings made use of healing plants.

It was natural that people would make use of what was to hand, whether this was to feed them, keep them warm or make them well. Finding cures for particular ailments was obviously carried out over the centuries on a trial and error basis. These cures were handed down by word of mouth, originally because this was the only way possible, but even with the spread of literacy family remedies continued to be handed on orally from generation to generation.

With the introduction of the National Health Service, people could consult doctors free of charge. This, in addition to the fact that many people had moved to populated urban areas where medical treatment was more readily available, and to the fact that transport facilities had generally increased, led to a marked decrease in the reliance of cures based on the fields, hedgerows and kitchen cupboards.

Recently there has been a reaction in society against our technological age, and some people are once again turning to simple, natural things and rejecting the sophisticated and the synthetic. This reaction has included remedies for illnesses, and herbal medicine has become popular as a branch of alternative medicine. To some extent the wheel has come full circle.

It should be pointed out that this book is intended only for the interest of the reader. It is in no way a do-it-yourself herbal manual and should not be treated as such. The whole area of folk and herbal medicine is one that is fraught with potential risk, some herbs being toxic and some being inappropriate, and even dangerous in certain situations. Anyone contemplating using herbal cures should consult a herbal specialist trained in modern herbal medicine techniques.

No one involved with the preparation or publication of the book can be held liable for any consequences arising from the use of this book or for any errors. This also applies to the old stain remedies given in the Appendix.

A

abdominal pains *see* **stomach pains**.

abrasions and cuts
Abrasions occur when the skin is grazed or broken slightly by scraping, rubbing or cutting.

Traditionally, cinnamon was used on abrasions as an antiseptic; clove oil was used to disinfect the wound; honey was spread on the wound to act as an antiseptic and to speed up the healing process; and tea was used externally to check bleeding and guard against infection.

Other common remedies included marigold flowers, crushed and applied externally; onion juice applied externally; crushed fresh parsley leaves; the crushed fresh leaves of plantain; a tea made from sage applied externally; dock leaves applied externally, either directly or in the form of a lotion; geranium leaves bruised and applied externally; and a poultice made of the pounded root or leaves of comfrey.

abscess

Yarrow, elderflowers and meadowsweet flowers were also used, as were compresses or poultices using witch hazel, and lavender was used while bathing. Later, iodine was much used on abrasions and cuts.

Other remedies were slightly more peculiar. One of these involved putting fresh elderflowers in an equal quantity of lard. This was then heated gently until the flowers were crisp and the mixture was strained through linen to form a kind of ointment. A similar ointment was made using lard and white horehound.

See also BLEEDING.

abscess

An abscess is a collection of pus, often occurring in a cavity and often causing an inflamed swelling.

There are several traditional cures for abscesses, some of them weirder than others. A common one, and one that was also used for boils, was the use of a hot poultice made from bread and milk to bring the abscess to a head.

Alternatively, a fresh egg was beaten with three tablespoonfuls of white flour and cooked slowly and carefully to form a white paste. This was then spread on a piece of cloth and applied to the affected area, the treatment being repeated every three hours.

Various herbs, used either separately or in combination, were also used in a poultice. These included chickweed, comfrey, marshmallow root, plantain, and slippery elm.

Vegetables were also used in the treatment of abscesses and boils. Raw carrots were used in hot poultices, as were crushed boiled turnips. A paste of mashed cooked leeks was spread on a piece of cloth and placed on the abscess or boil, and onion juice was applied externally. Eucalyptus oil was also used.

It seems highly unlikely that many us of will try out one traditional remedy in particular. This involved taking a quantity of snails and boiling them in ground salt before applying the resultant paste to the area affected by the abscess or boil.

See also BOILS.

acidity

Acidity of the stomach manifests itself in bouts of heartburn and indigestion.

A cure for this consisted of a small amount of bicarbonate of soda in a glass of fairly hot water. Another cure consisted of putting two teaspoonfuls of magnesia in a tumbler of milk.

Sometimes, however, acidity of the stomach was treated not with antacids but with acidic substances. One cure prescribed two teaspoonfuls of cider vinegar mixed with one teaspoonful of lemon juice and one teaspoonful of potato juice.

acne

Acne is a chronic skin complaint in which blackheads and pustules appear on the face and other parts of the body, commonly the back. It is a disorder of the sebaceous glands, which produce sebum that, in its normal amounts, keeps the skin supple and elastic.

When the channel through which the sebum reaches the surface becomes blocked, the dead cells forming the blockage can turn black, hence causing the blackheads. If the blocked gland situated at the base of the blockage becomes infected, a reddened inflamed spot may develop.

Acne is particularly common among adolescents because of hormonal activity on reaching puberty. Severe acne, especially if it goes untreated, can leave scarring and pockmarks on the area that has been affected.

Older, more traditional remedies for acne included using various herbs as a facial steam. One of these steams consisted of chickweed, elderflower and marigold, used in equal parts. Agrimony applied externally was also thought to be curative.

Another remedy involved the spreading of sulphur ointment over the affected areas.

Nowadays there are various abrasive substances on the market to remove blackheads, but an older remedy involved applying a watch key over the offending blackhead and pressing. People still squeeze blackheads by pressing them, although not generally with watch keys.

It is best not to squeeze infected blackheads, however, in case this makes them worse.

There is often said to be a dietary factor in acne, although many doctors feel that there is no evidence for this. Thus, some remedies were designed to be taken internally. Aperients generally were recommended.

Another internal cure involved mixing two ounces of clover flowers, two ounces of nettle tops and two ounces of comfrey flowers with four pints of boiling water and simmering this until only two pints were left. A wineglass of the resulting liquid was to be taken every three hours.

adder's tongue, English

Common names for this commonly found plant are serpent's tongue and Christ's spear. In traditional herbal remedies it was used as an emetic. It was also used to speed up wound healing and for sore eyes. Another use was to soothe and soften the skin. It was administered either as a poultice or in the form of an infusion

adenoids, inflammation of

Adenoids are fleshy growths at the back of the nose. When they became enlarged or inflamed, a common traditional remedy was to make a solution of salt and water and sniff it up the nose.

Alternatively, a solution of one teaspoonful of salt in

warm water was used as a gargle. This is in fact often used as a gargle for sore throats today.

ageing

People have long looked for the elixir of youth, but it is still absolutely certain that, unless we die prematurely, we will all undergo the ageing process, although it is more obvious earlier in some people than in others.

Various traditional methods were used to try to slow down the ageing process. In China, ginseng was used as an aid to longevity and an aid to a good memory in old age. Nearer home, a tea made from comfrey, drunk on a regular basis, was thought to promote health in old age.

Ginger was also thought to slow down the ageing process, and in recent times it has indeed been shown to have antioxidant properties, which are discussed below. Rosemary was thought to improve the memory, which often deteriorates in old age. In Ayurvedic medicine, myrrh is believed to rejuvenate the body and the mind and even to reverse the ageing process.

Recent research has shown that some of the products long used in home remedies are high in antioxidants, which neutralize destructive free radicals and may be instrumental in helping to alleviate various degenerative diseases and in retarding the ageing process. Some of these products include lemon, potatoes, wheat-germ, carrots, olive oil, ginger and rosemary.

agrimony

Popular names for agrimony are church steeples, because of the shape of its tall flower spikes, and sticklewort.

In medieval times agrimony was said to possess magical powers that could ward off the powers of witchcraft. It was especially valued as a cure for insomnia. The story was that if you put some agrimony under your head when you went to sleep, you would sleep so soundly that you appeared to be dead and that you would not wake until the agrimony was taken from under your head.

It was also believed to have the ability to draw out splinters embedded in the flesh, and when used in a poultice was supposed to alleviate bites and stings. Acne was also thought to be cured by it.

Indeed, the plant was considered to be so versatile that it was regarded as a sovereign remedy. It was thought to have a beneficial effect on the liver, kidneys and bladder and was used as a diuretic.

Agrimony was also used as an expectorant in cases of persistent coughing and as a herbal gargle. It was also used as a preventative for diarrhoea and as an astringent and tonic—a plant with wide-ranging powers indeed.

ague

Ague is a term that we do not use any more. It was once used to describe any disease that brought on a fever

hellebore – the roots of the hellebore were used to cure ague

accompanied by shivering of the kind that occurs in influenza. Later it was used to describe malarial fever.

A traditional cure for ague or malarial fever was to treat it with an infusion of marigold flowers. Alternatively, an ointment made with the crushed leaves of elder was used. Bryony was used when other remedies failed, although this had to be used with extreme caution since it is very poisonous.

Other cures for ague, probably in its more general sense, were not so commonplace. One old cure was rather complex. It involved the gathering together of equal quantities of tobacco dust and soot, and nine cloves of garlic. These ingredients were then beaten together and mixed with soap to make a stiff paste that was then shaped into two cakes. These were laid on the inside of each wrist of the ague victim, being bound on with rags, and were supposed to be applied one hour before the next fit was expected — how the timing was reckoned is not made clear. If this treatment was not effective the first time round, it was to be repeated in three or four days time.

There was an alternative cure, but whether this was in any way preferable is hard to say. For this, the person intent on effecting a cure had to acquire a pennyworth (whatever that entailed in the middle of the eighteenth century) of black soap, a pennyworth of gunpowder, an ounce of tobacco snuff and a glass of brandy. This mixture was to be mixed thoroughly in a mortar and spread on pieces of leather fastened onto the wrists. Again, these were to be applied an hour before the fit was expected.

The person working out the timing of the next fit of ague had an even greater problem with yet another potential cure current in the middle of the eighteenth century. This had to be applied six hours before the next fit was expected and involved mixing Venice turpentine with the powder of white hellebore roots until it was stiff enough to spread on pieces of leather. These were then laid on the wrists and over the balls of the thumbs.

Ague seems to have attracted more than its fair share of cures. Another remedy involved the patient fasting seven mornings in a row but for eating seven sage leaves.

Another suggestion was that the person suffering from ague should bury a handful of salt in the ground in the hope that his or her ague would disappear as the salt dissolved.

If you disliked someone very much, such as a neighbour, you got revenge by trying to infect him or her with your ague in a strange way. The theory was that the ague sufferer would bury under the doorstep of the neighbour's house a bag that contained the parings from a dead man's nails and some hairs from his head—although whether these would be readily available seems unlikely.

Traditionally, charms were popular to ward off disease. At least they must have seemed preferable to the cures. In the case of ague, people wishing to avoid the disease were encouraged to put a tansy leaf in their shoes.

In an early attempt at preventative medicine people were also encouraged to take a pill made from a spider's web to ward off ague. One of these pills was to be taken each morning before breakfast.

albumen water

To make albumen water, the white of an absolutely new-laid egg was separated from the yolk and whisked until it was a stiff froth. It was then added to half a pint of cold water and the mixture was them left covered with a saucer for an hour so that the egg white dissolved. A dash of lemon juice or a pinch of salt could be added if desired.

Albumen water was used for diarrhoea or digestive problems.

alcohol

Alcohol baths were sometimes given to patients who were in the beginning stages of pleurisy to try to get him or her to perspire freely.

Alcohol was applied to wounds to act as an astringent to stop bleeding and also to prevent infection. Because of its skin-hardening properties, it was applied to bed sores and to sore nipples in breast-feeding mothers. As a liniment it was used as a counterirritant for rheumatism and arthritis.

It was taken internally to relieve pain and was applied to teeth and gums to bring temporary relief from toothache.

alder

The bark and leaves of alder contain tannic acid and were used traditionally as a tonic and as an astringent.

aloes

The bark or leaves were boiled and the resultant liquid used to bathe areas of swelling and to reduce inflammation, particularly of the throat.

aloes

Aloes was traditionally used as a purgative and as a cure for parasitic worms. It was also used to stimulate the menstrual discharge.

alopecia *see* **baldness**.

alum

Alum was traditionally used in France as a treatment for chilblains on the hands. A small piece was taken and melted in enough hot water to cover the hands. After the alum was melted, the chilblain-sufferer put his or her hands in the liquid and covered the hands with gloves. These were to be kept on all night and as long as possible during the day.

Alum was also used to alleviate the effects of excessive perspiration.

anaemia

This was sometimes informally known as bloodlessness and is a condition in which there is a lack of red blood corpuscles, or haemoglobin, caused either by inadequate production of red blood cells or prolonged loss of blood.

Traditional cures for anaemia include nettle tea, which is rich in iron, often sweetened with some honey, or dandelion tea. Alternatively, an infusion of herbs could be taken, the herbs including alfalfa, centaury, dandelion root, rose-hip, watercress and yellow dock, both nettle and yellow dock being exceptionally high in iron content.

Watercress, being rich in iron, was also used as a cure for anaemia, as were wheat, carrots, cabbage, onions and apples. Comfrey was also an ancient cure for anaemia, and angelica, barberry, fenugreek, fumitory, St John's wort and vervain were also used in treatment.

anenome, meadow

Another common name is pasqueflower. The whole plant was used in traditional herbal remedies.

It was used in the treatment of asthma, bronchitis, whooping cough and respiratory diseases generally. Disorders of the digestive system were also treated with it, as were some nervous problems.

angelica

Angelica was once thought to have magical powers, It was thought to have the power to protect anyone using it from the powers of darkness.

It is now chiefly used in crystallized form in cake decoration, but it was used widely in folk medicine. The roots were thought to be able to ward off infection, and in the

angelica

Great Plague of 1665 many Londoners chewed pieces of angelica root in the belief that it would prevent them from catching the disease.

The plant was also used to stimulate the appetite. Flatulence and indigestion were also thought to be helped by it.

Angelica was also used as an expectorant in respiratory disorders, being used to alleviate colds, coughs, sore throats, influenza, and bronchitis. It was also used to bring down fevers.

It was thought to have extremely wide-ranging powers, being also useful in the treatment of urinary disorders and disorders of the kidneys. Muscular cramps and chilblains were also treated with it.

This is an impressive range of treatments, but these

were not all. The plant was also thought to be instrumental in improving bad eyesight and deafness.

ankle, sprained *see* sprains.

ankles, weak

Some illnesses, such as scarlet fever, were thought to
leave the patient with weak ankles after the illness was
cured. A cure that would now seem rather exotic involved oysters. The patient was advised to take a raw
oyster in the palm of the right hand and massage the
ankles with it until the oyster was more or less rubbed
into nonexistence. This practice was to be carried out
every evening before the sufferer went to bed and was
to be carried on until the ankles grew stronger.

ammonia

Ammonia was sometimes used in cold cures. It was inhaled in the way that menthol was, and still is.

It was also used to treat feet that perspired excessively.
The feet were washed with ammonia and then they were
rubbed with ammonia, particularly between the toes.
Tired feet could be bathed in water containing ammonia and bay rum.

Ammonia was also used in the treatment of stings
and bites. It was used to alleviate bites made by ants,
gnats and mosquitoes.

antiseptics

Various herbs were known for their antiseptic powers in folk and herbal medicine. These included avens, costmary, garlic, oak, thyme, violet and woundwort.

antidotes *see* poison, antidotes to.

anxiety

There were various herbs and plants that were noted for their calming effect on the nerves in folk medicine. These included balm, catnip, chamomile, cloves, hawthorn, hops, lavender, lime flowers, orange blossom, passiflora, skullcap, thyme, valerian, vervain and wood betony.

aperients

An aperient is a mild type of laxative for evacuating the bowels. Herbs used as aperients in folk and herbal medicine included clary, club moss, costmary, couchgrass, dandelion, elder, feverfew, marigold, marshmallow, parsley and rhubarb.

aphrodisiac

Honey and ginger were both considered by the ancients to be aphrodisiacs. Onions were also considered to have aphrodisiac qualities, and one custom involved the giving of onion soup to couples on their wedding night.

Celery, dill, fennel, hawthorn, nettle, valerian and watercress were also once considered to have aphrodisiac qualities. Nowadays, some people consider oysters to be aphrodisiac.

appetite, lack of

One traditional remedy for lack of appetite involved making a drink from a handful of hops and caraway seeds. This was particularly recommended for loss of appetite following a debilitating illness.

Watercress and angelica were also thought to stimulate the appetite, as was barley. Carrots, too, were thought to encourage people to eat.

Herbs that were considered to be appetite stimulants included chamomile, lavender, sage, thyme, tarragon, marjoram, yarrow, hawthorn, myrrh, centaury, gentian, hops and wormwood. Horseradish was also used to encourage people to eat.

apple

Apples were long thought to be exceptionally health-giving. Modern medical research seems to back up the old adage 'An apple a day keeps the doctor away' by revealing that apples and apple juice can be powerful tools against viruses.

The apple had many uses in traditional medicine. Its medicinal advantages have been recognized since the times of the ancient Greeks and Romans. In Greek mythology the apple, which was said to taste like honey, was regarded virtually as a cure-all.

Apples were thought to be good for complaints relating to the digestive system. They were thought to be useful both as a laxative and as a treatment for diarrhoea, as well as helping to regulate acidity in the stomach.

The liver, gall bladder and urinary problems were all said to be helped by the intake of apples. They were used as a cure for fluid retention.

Cooked apples were thought to be helpful in cases of insomnia by promoting a restful sleep. They were also thought to act as a sedative and to relieve anxiety.

Other disorders that apples were meant to be able to help were arthritis, gout and headaches. Heart problems, anaemia, lethargy, influenza, fever and decongestion were all thought to be alleviated by the eating of apples. It is obvious why the apple was regarded as a general panacea.

Apples were regarded as dampeners of the appetite but were used in some invalid drinks. These included apple water, which was made by slicing two large apples and pouring two pints of boiling water on them. This was then allowed to stand for two hours and was then strained.

Apple tea was made by roasting two large sour apples and covering them with boiling water. The resulting mixture was allowed to cool and was then strained.

Baked apples were used externally for a number of complaints. They were used in earache and, when mashed with some sulphur, they were used on the skin to cure scabies and ringworm. Mixed with a little olive oil, baked apples were used on wounds that were proving difficult to heal.

Grated raw apple was used in a poultice for sore eyes and, also in a poultice, was used as a cure for varicose veins.

arnica

Arnica is commonly called mountain tobacco or leopard's bane.

It was, and often still is, applied externally in the form of poultices or lotion to alleviate bruises and sprains. Arnica was also used internally as a diuretic and stimulant, but it frequently irritated the stomach and in some cases could lead to quite severe poisoning

arthritis

Arthritis is a painful condition in which the joints are inflamed. It is a difficult condition to treat, and many of the modern treatments have side effects.

Various ways of alleviating the condition were popular in folk or herbal medicine. As one would expect, some of them involved poultices.

One of these had as its ingredient fresh ragwort leaves.

Another poultice was made from a handful of coltsfoot boiled in milk with oats and butter. Cabbage was also used in poultices to reduce inflammation, and the leaves and flowers of borage were also used in the same way.

Cloves were added to alcohol to make a liniment to rub on painful joints, as was thyme. The bruised fresh leaves of peppermint were applied to painful joints also, and in China eucalyptus oil was used in this way.

Various infusions and teas were also recommended as folk cures. One of these was made from a teacupful of honeysuckle flowers and a pint of boiling water. Mustard seeds in an infusion was another suggested cure

Another herbal tea thought to alleviate arthritis was more complicated. It required agrimony, bogbean, burdock and yarrow in equal quantities with about one quarter of the amount of raspberry leaves. This was to be added to boiling water and reduced to half the original amount of liquid. It was then allowed to cool and was strained. Again, a wineglass of the liquid was to be taken every three hours.

Cinnamon, watercress, vinegar, apple, carrots, leeks, onions, turnip, parsley, dandelion leaves, nettle leaves, dock, marigold, lemon juice and cucumber taken internally were also recommended for the relief of arthritis.

Other herbs that were thought to alleviate the symptoms included buckthorn, chickweed, rosemary, sage, comfrey, mistletoe, meadowsweet, rue, wintergreen and wormwood.

An Epsom salts bath taken once or twice a week was once recommended for arthritis sufferers

ash

The bark and leaves of ash were used as laxatives and purgatives, often in association with other purgatives, such as senna or rhubarb.

Ash could also be used as a tonic for invalids and was thought to prevent the return of recurring diseases, such as malaria.

asthma

Asthma is a respiratory disorder. People suffering from a bout of asthma find it difficult to breathe properly. Muscular spasm makes it difficult for them to get rid of mucus by coughing.

Much concern is being expressed about asthma today but, of course, it is by no means a new disease. There were several folk remedies that were given to try and alleviate the symptoms. One old country remedy was for sufferers of asthma to drink a pint of cold water every morning. They were also advised to take a cold bath every morning.

Not all remedies advised the drinking of water. Another one advised the drinking of apple water, which is described under apple.

Yet another remedy puts its faith in a drink made from liquorice. An ounce of stick liquorice was cut into slices. This was soaked in a quart of water and was to be drunk when the asthma sufferer was having a worse bout than usual. Another remedy advocated drinking a pint of new milk every morning and evening.

An infusion made with agrimony was also recommended. Another drink involved slicing one pound of sliced garlic, macerating it in a dish containing two pints of boiling water and leaving it for twelve hours. The liquid was then strained and sugar was added. One teaspoonful of this liquid was to be taken.

Another folk cure involved boiling equal quantities of caraway seeds and fennel seeds in vinegar. Some garlic was then added, and when the liquid had cooled and been strained, honey was added. A teaspoonful of this was to be taken as required.

A teaspoon of chopped thyme was also recommended for the relief of symptoms of asthma. A small amount of lemon juice taken in water before a meal was also thought to be of help, as was cider vinegar. Tea also was held to have curative powers with regard to asthma, and a tea made from rosemary was thought to relieve the bronchial spasm common in asthma.

Carrots taken internally were thought to have expectorant properties. Because of this, people suffering from asthma were advised to eat carrots in order to expel mucus. Plantain was also noted as an expectorant to get rid of mucus and was used as such in cases of asthma, as were sage and eucalyptus. Nettle was thought to reduce the congestion in asthma, and myrrh was regarded as a decongestant and as an expectorant for getting rid of phlegm.

A decoction of parsley seeds, noted for their power to relax muscle, was also thought to relieve asthma, as was hyssop. Thyme was considered to have the ability to relax the bronchial tubes and also to get rid of phlegm by its expectorant properties. Elderflowers were held to be effective in reducing congestion and also in relieving spasm.

Asthma sufferers were also advised to inhale the steam from a combination of boiling water and chamomile.

Food that was easily digestible was recommended. Eating ripe fruits, whether baked, boiled or roasted, was meant to be good for asthma. An alternative form of food advocated for asthma was thin bread and butter spread with minced garlic. Somewhat less palatable was something else recommended to be eaten as a cure for asthma. This was a handful of spider webs rolled into a ball.

Other herbs thought to be useful in the treatment of

asthma included burdock, butterbur, horseradish, lovage, mullein, valerian and white horehound.

asparagus

Asparagus is best known to most of us as a vegetable, since its fleshy young shoots are used in cooking. Its root, however, was also valued for its medicinal properties. It was noted as a laxative and was also used to induce the flow of urine. It was recommended in the treatment of fluid retention, kidney disorders, gout, rheumatic pains and as a sedative. Heart disease was also treated with it.

The asparagus root was sometimes used in an infusion, and sometimes the expressed juice was used. Early herbalists claimed that asparagus was a cure for impotence.

athlete's foot

Athlete's foot is a fungal infection of the feet, being usually found between the toes.

Vinegar was considered to be effective against fungal infections and was commonly used in cases of athlete's foot. Clove oil, being a natural disinfectant, was also used.

Garlic was also used in the treatment of athlete's foot. Sometimes crushed garlic was used, sometimes it was sliced and macerated in oil, and sometimes it was made into an ointment.

People suffering from athlete's foot were sometimes advised to bathe their feet in a decoction of burdock. Some drops of eucalyptus oil were mixed with almond oil or olive oil and applied to the skin directly.

avens

Some common names for avens include colewort, herb bennet, wild rue and clove root. The herb itself and the root were thought to have medicinal properties.

Avens in traditional herbal medicine was considered useful as an antiseptic and as a tonic. It was also used to check bleeding, to reduce fever and induce perspiration.

Avens was used in the treatment of stomach complaints, such as colic, and in the treatment of diarrhoea. Headache, sore throats and chills were also treated with it, and it was used in heart disease and disorders of the liver.

It was used externally to remove blemishes and spots and relieve skin conditions. Another use was as a gargle and mouthwash

Because it is a strong aromatic it was once alleged to have the power to drive away evil spirits. It was once believed that anyone carrying a sprig of avens would not be bitten by a rabid dog or by a poisonous snake. It was once held to be an antidote to poison and animal bites.

avens

Another piece of folklore advised that if someone dug up the root of an avens plant before sunrise and hung it in a linen bag round the neck it would improve the eyesight. The same strange practice was also once thought to be a cure for piles.

B

backache

An old remedy for backache involved making a poultice from hot aniseed and nettle leaves and applying it to the painful area of the back.

Another cure involved massaging with comfrey oil.
See also SCIATICA.

baldness

There were various traditional remedies designed either to prevent or cure baldness. These were recommended also in the cases of bald patches, known as alopecia.

One suggested preventative was washing the hair once a week at least in water containing an egg yolk or a piece of quillia bark. This was particularly recommended during periods of ill-health, when people were thought to be particularly susceptible to baldness.

To stimulate the hair follicles it was suggested that a few drops of cantharides were added to vinegar. This was used to wash the hair and was also rubbed on the scalp.

An alternative recommendation was a mixture of onion juice and honey. This was to be rubbed on the scalp every morning and evening.

The regular application of a mixture of glycerine and lime water, or a mixture of olive oil and lime water, was another suggested remedy. This was thought to be effective in the case of hair that was already showing signs of thinning.

Those whose heads were already quite bald were advised to try to revive the roots of the hair that was still there by brushing the scalp until it was red and felt warm. Then a lotion consisting of lavender oil, rosemary oil, eau de Cologne and tincture of cantharides was applied to the head once or twice daily. Alternatively, a mixture of rosemary oil and olive oil was advised as a massage for the scalp.

balm

Popular names for this herb include lemon balm, sweet balm and cure-all.

Balm was noted for its supposed powers to break fevers and encourage perspiration, and was thus a recommended cure for all feverish illnesses. It was also used to treat colds, influenza, catarrh and hay fever. Balm was thought to be effective in the treatment of flatulence and digestive disorders, and was considered to be a remedy for menstrual cramps. Headaches and dizziness were treated with it, as was high blood pressure.

It was used to raise the spirits of people who were depressed, particularly menopausal women, to allay anxiety and to improve concentration. It supposedly also improved poor memories. Balm tea was sometimes given to listless or lazy children in an effort to stimulate them.

Externally it was used to dress wounds, to bring boils to a head and to relieve insect stings. It was used to treat eczema, inflammation of the eye and as a gargle for sore throats.

barberry

This woodland plant is often known as sowberry.

In ancient Egypt barberry was used in combination with fennel seeds as a cure for the plague.

Later it was used as a purgative and was used in cures for dysentery. Barberry contains berberine, which has astringent properties, and was commonly used in gargles and mouth washes as a cure for sore throats. Other disorders thought to be helped by it were high blood pressure and kidney stones. Barberry is high in vitamin C.

barley

In ancient Greece and ancient Rome barley was used to increase vitality and build up strength. It is easily digested and is highly nutritious, and was much used in soup or gruel to try to tempt patients' appetites and thus help bring them back to full strength. Digestive and bowel upsets, such as colic, diarrhoea, and constipation, loss of appetite and nervous disorders were also treated by it.

Barley water was also used in the treatment of respiratory disorders, being thought to help disorders of the lungs, to relieve sore chests and to ease dry coughs. It was also used to treat cystitis and other disorders of the urinary system.

This was made by adding a tablespoonful of pearl barley to a pint of water that was then boiled, although quantities varied. The boiled water was then drained off and a pint and a half of clean water added. The barley and water were then simmered gently and strained. Sugar and lemon could be added if desired.

Barley flour could be used in poultices. Such poultices were applied to the skin to soothe inflammation.

basil

Most of us think of basil, also sometimes known as sweet basil, as a herb used in cooking. However, it was also used in herbal medicine.

In the Middle Ages basil was used to relieve the pains of women in labour. It was also thought to be able to draw out the poison from scorpion stings.

It was later used as a cure for various ailments. Nausea, vomiting, and stomach cramps were thought to be alleviated by it, as were obstructions of the internal organs and constipation.

Headaches were also said to be soothed by basil, and it was used to relieve insomnia. Vertigo and dizziness were thought to be cured by it, as were mild nervous disorders. Usually administered as an infusion, the herb was said to have the power to increase the flow of breast milk in nursing mothers.

Oil of basil was recommended for treating insect stings, bites and minor cuts and abrasions.

bearberry
Sometimes called bear's grape, bearberry was used in early Welsh folk medicine as an antiseptic.

Later it was commonly used to promote the flow of urine and in kidney and urinary disorders, such as cystitis. It turns the urine green. Prolonged use of bearberry resulted in constipation.

bed sores
Alcohol was rubbed on bed sores to harden the skin and to alleviate the condition. Witch hazel was also used, either in the form of a poultice or in the form of a compress.

bed-wetting
One particularly unpleasant early remedy for bed-wet-

ting was to give the child boiled mouse flesh. Practically anything would be more palatable than that.

Another early remedy, fortunately a great deal less gruesome, was a tea made from St John's wort and plantain and sweetened with honey. Also more pleasant was a mixture of thyme and honey.

An infusion of various herbs was also recommended, the herbs being basil, betony, golden rod and tansy. A later remedy involved the use of cardamom. This was also used in cases of incontinence.

Other herbs thought to be useful for curing bed-wetting were bearbery, fennel, hollyhock, pansy and St John's wort.

One rather strange suggestion related to the way the child lay in bed. To prevent children who persistently wet the bed from so doing, it was recommended that they were discouraged from sleeping on their backs by taping an empty cotton reel to the back of their nightwear. This was also used in an attempt to stop people from snoring.

beef tea

Beef tea was much used in cases of debility or convalescence where the strength of patients had to be built up. There were various methods of making this. One method involved mincing or cutting up beefsteak and then putting it in a jar or dish with a pint and a half of cold water or barley water. The jar was covered, placed in a saucepan of water and simmered for several hours. Alternatively, the container was placed in a cool oven overnight. The contents were then strained and the fat removed.

belladonna

Belladonna is better known to most of us as deadly nightshade. It is extremely poisonous and, although it was used in the treatment of several disorders, it was also known to result in accidental poisoning or even death.

It was used in the relief of pain, as in cases of sciatica, rheumatism, bunions and toothache. The plant was also used as a sedative and to relieve fever. Belladonna was also used as a diuretic in cases of fluid retention.

Eye disorders were commonly treated with it. Belladonna makes the pupils of the eyes dilate.

betony

This woodland plant was once thought to confer protection against evil and sorcery. It was also believed that if betony was planted in churchyards it would prevent the spirits of the dead from appearing at night.

In early times the plant was thought to be an antidote to snakebites and to be a cure for the bites of rabid dogs. Another early theory was that it would cure drunkenness if it were gathered by means other than by using an iron implement.

Later, betony was thought to have a number of uses.

bilberry

It was used in the treatment of neuralgia and headaches, and as a cure for heartburn, high blood pressure, gallstones and kidney infections. Betony was used as a tonic, a sedative and a treatment for excessive sweating. It was also thought to cure the spitting up of blood.

The plant was commonly administered as an infusion. When used externally it was said to be effective in the treatment of boils, sores and cuts.

bilberry

Bilberry is also commonly known as whortleberry, blueberry, blaeberry and whinberry. The ripe fruits and leaves had various uses in folk medicine.

The fruit was used as a diuretic in cases of fluid retention and was also thought to be effective in other urinary disorders. Diarrhoea, dysentery and other bowel complaints were also treated with the fruit of the bilberry. Bilberry was also used in the treatment of scurvy.

The leaves of the plant were used in the same way as bearberry.

biliousness

One suggested remedy for a bilious attack was to take a glass of hot water containing lemon juice before retiring for the night. Another involved drinking a small cup of coffee containing lemon juice and a pinch of salt, fasting for a period of twenty-four hours and then eating only raw apples for the next period of twenty-four hours.

Epsom salts were also thought to be helpful in the treatment of biliousness. Another remedy advocated washing out the stomach with large quantities of water or soda water and taking purgatives. Thereafter fasting was advocated.

birch

The bark and leaves of the birch tree were used in herbal medicine. Skin diseases were treated with an ointment made from an oil made from birch bark.

The leaves were made into a tea and used as a remedy for gout, dropsy, breaking up kidney stones and rheumatism.

birthwort

The root of the birthwort was once used to clear obstructions after childbirth. It was also used in the treatment of gout and rheumatism.

bites and stings *see* stings and bites.

bittersweet

A common name for bittersweet is woody nightshade. The twigs and root bark were used in herbal medicine.

It was used as a diuretic in cases of fluid retention and

disorders of the kidneys. Disorders of the skin and catarrh, bronchitis, asthma and whooping cough were also thought to respond to bittersweet.

blackberry

Blackberry is commonly known, particularly in Scotland, as bramble. The root and leaves were used in herbal medicine. It was used to treat dysentery, diarrhoea and piles.

Whooping cough was also treated with blackberry, as were feverish colds.

blackcurrant

The fruit, leaves, bark and root of the blackcurrant bush were used traditionally in herbal medicine. Blackcurrant was used as a diuretic in cases of fluid retention. It was used in feverish illnesses to reduce and break the fever. Other uses included the reduction of swelling and the cure of haemorrhoids or piles.

It was also used as a general tonic and as a gargle.

blackhead *see* acne.

black pepper *see* pepper.

bladder, irritable

A decoction of parsley seeds was used in the treatment of an irritable bladder. Yarrow was also used.

bleeding

In folk medicine there were various recommended cures for bleeding. Yarrow was a very early one. The Greek hero Achilles is said to have used it to stop the bleeding from the wounds of his companions.

The application of a cobweb was a well-known cure for bleeding. Sometimes this was accompanied by a dressing of brown sugar placed on a piece of cloth.

Powdered rice placed on a piece of cloth and applied to the bleeding area was thought to be an effective cure. Sometimes a handful of flour was sprinkled over the wound to try and stop it bleeding or a dry dressing made of flour and salt.

Cinnamon was thought to reduce or stop bleeding, particularly in the case of nose bleeding or heavy periods. Lemon juice was recommended for bleeding gums or for applying to the nostrils in the case of nose bleeds.

Vinegar was applied to wounds to reduce bleeding, and alcohol was used in the same way. Tea, because of its astringent properties, was also used, as were witch hazel and eucalyptus oil.

Plantain applied externally was thought to be able to reduce bleeding, as were rosemary leaves applied externally. Nettle leaves were also used, as were marigold flowers or leaves and meadowsweet flowers.

Comfrey taken internally was also used to stem

bleeding, being also used externally for bleeding gums. Rose taken internally was another cure.

One older cure involved some advance action. In the month of May people were advised to take a piece of cloth and wet it in frog spawn for nine days, drying it off each day in the wind. Pieces of the cloth could then be used to stem bleeding, as the need arose.

See also NOSE.

blisters

A poultice of cabbage leaves was one remedy that was used for the relief of blisters. Crushed dock leaves applied to the blisters were also thought to soothe them and to help to heal them.

A cure for blistered feet recommended using a mixture of salicylic acid, starch and pulverized soapstone. This was to be applied to socks or stockings and shoes. The remedy was also advised for swollen feet.

blood clots

Ginger was used to prevent excessive blood clotting, as was cayenne pepper. Garlic was used to counteract a tendency for blood to clot too much, and olive oil was thought to reduce the risk of blood clots. Onions were used to thin the blood and dissolve blood clots, and broom was sometimes used as an anticoagulant.

bloodlessness *see* **anaemia**.

blood pressure, high *see* **hypertension**.

blood pressure, low *see* **hypotension**.

blushing
A suggested old cure for excessive blushing involved taking half a wine-glassful of an infusion containing gentian.

gentian – used to cure blushing

body odour
Before the days of patent deodorants and antiperspirants, it was suggested that body odours could be kept at bay by washing twice a day with carbolic soap or coal tar

soap and then dusting oneself with boracic acid. It was also suggested that socks and stockings should be dipped in a boracic lotion before being hung up to dry.

People who perspired a great deal were advised to use a little ammonia in the bath.

See also PERSPIRATION.

bogbean

Bogbean is a plant that had various uses in herbal medicine. It was used as a tonic and to reduce fever. Constipation and obstruction of the bowels were also thought to be relieved by bogbean.

The plant was used to treat rheumatism and skin complaints and to reduce glandular swelling. In some areas bogbean was used in the treatment of stomach complaints, particularly ulcers.

bones, broken

Comfrey was used to speed the knitting of broken bones.

boneset

Boneset is a plant of the daisy family, also known as feverwort and Indian sage.

It was used to treat the common cold, catarrh and influenza. In addition, it was regarded as being a tonic, an expectorant to bring up phlegm, a laxative, a stimulant and as a means of bringing down fevers.

Disorders of the bowel, stomach, liver, bowel and uterus were treated by it, as were some skin diseases.

boils

There were various old methods for bringing a boil to a head. One of these was the application of a flour and treacle poultice. Another one, and one that sounds agonizing, involved heating a glass jar with very hot water, pouring the water out of the jar, and placing the hot jar on the boil.

Poultices were made from watercress, lemon balm or honey and applied to the boil. More usual poultices made from bread and milk were also used to bring boils to a head. To draw the boil a paste of mashed cooked leeks was applied, and grated raw carrot was used in a poultice to speed up the healing process.

Onion juice was also used to cure boils, as was a poultice made from crushed boiled turnips. A burdock poultice could be used to reduce inflammation and a comfrey hot poultice to draw the pus. A compress using eucalyptus oil was thought to be effective in speeding the healing process. Horseradish was also used externally as a cure for boils.

Another folk cure to bring a boil to a head used an egg. The egg was boiled and the skin peeled from it while it was still wet. The skin was then placed on the boil.

borage

Boils were also cured using Epsom salts. Sufferers from boils were advised to put some Epsom salts in a dish and place it in an oven until it became powdery. A little glycerine was then added and the mixture put on a piece of cloth or lint and placed on the boil.

Haricot beans were used in a cure for boils. The haricot beans were reduced to a powder and mixed with fenu-greek and honey before being applied to the boil.

A simpler and more pleasant method used chamomile flowers. These were used in hot fomentations that were applied to the boil.

Some remedies were internal. A drink was made from the root of the dock plant and boiling water and taken to purify the blood. Alternatively, the centres of blackberry shoots were boiled, left to soak and strained. The resultant liquid was to be drunk every morning.

Boils were thought to be a sign that the sufferer was not in the best of health. Tonics and purgatives were recommended.

See also ABSCESS.

borage

Borage in medieval times was thought to promote courage. From early times it was thought also to have a cheering influence on people.

In herbal medicine it was used in many ways. As well as lifting the spirits, it was thought to have the ability to quieten palpitations and to restore energy during a period of convalescence. It was used also to increase the production of sweat and as a diuretic in cases of fluid retention.

The symptoms of respiratory infections were also treated with it, as it relieved congestion and helped to bring up phlegm. Borage was used in the treatment of sore throats, chest infections, bronchitis and tracheitis.

A poultice made with the leaves and flowers of borage was used to relieve skin conditions, such as eczema and ringworm. A poultice made with borage was wrapped round painful joints in arthritis and gout.

Borage was used to make gargles and mouthwashes to treat sore throats, laryngitis or bleeding gums.

The leaves and seeds of borage were given to nursing mothers to increase their milk supply.

breast-feeding

Carrots were taken by nursing mothers to increase their milk supply. Parsley was taken to achieve the same effect, as were nettles. The leaves and seeds of borage were also thought to increase the flow of milk in nursing mothers.

breasts, soreness of

An old treatment for the relief of painful, swollen breasts, in nursing mothers, was the eating of sprouted barley, which was thought to dry up the milk. Crushed fresh parsley leaves applied externally were also thought to relieve engorgement of breasts when breast-feeding. A poultice or compress using witch hazel was supposed to relieve breast engorgement.

Sore breasts or nipples were thought to be relieved by the application of a mixture of groundsel and daisies. A poultice made from chamomile flowers and bruised marshmallow roots was also said to bring relief.

An ointment could be made from alum, sugar, vinegar and salt. This was simmered and spread on a piece of cloth that was applied to the area of the sore breast.

A drink made of vervain, betony and agrimony was also said to relieve breast pain. The herbs were crushed and mixed with beer and boiling milk.

breathlessness

Hawthorn was used to treat breathlessness, particularly when it was a symptom of heart disease.

A mixture of caraway seeds, aniseed, nutmeg, liquorice and sugar was recommended for shortness of breath. This mixture was crushed and a pinch of it was to be taken every morning and evening.

bronchitis

Many herbs were used in the treatment of bronchitis. These included angelica, borage, bugle, butterbur, caraway, chervil, chickweed, coltsfolt and comfrey. Daisy, fennel, fenugreek, garlic, ground ivy, knotgrass, liquorice, madder, myrrh, marjoram were other herbs that were commonly used in the treatment of bronchitis.

Other herbs that were thought to bring relief to sufferers from bronchitis were mullein, onion, parsley, plantain, primrose and sage. Savory, speedwell, thyme, watercress and white horehound were also used as treatments for bronchitis.

Cinnamon, honey, ginger, and tea were used a bronchial treatments, as was eucalyptus. Carrot and turnip were also used.

chickweed – used to treat bronchitis

broom

Broom is a shrub that was used in medieval times. Herbalists used to mix the ashes of burnt broom with white wine to cure fluid retention.

In more recent times it continued to be used as a diuretic. It was also used in remedies for kidney, bladder and liver disorders. Gout and sciatica were also treated with it.

Broom was also used in cases of excessive menstrual flow and was an anticoagulant. It was used to treat low blood pressure and sometimes heart disease. However, it had to be used with great caution, since it could adversely affect the heart or respiratory system and even cause death.

bruises

There were many remedies in folk medicine for the treatment of bruises.

A local application of vinegar was once a popular cure for a bruise. Alternatively, vinegar could be used in a poultice made from bran and breadcrumbs or oatmeal. This was applied to bruises and sprains.

Water was used in some suggested remedies. One of these advocated wrapping the bruised area with cloths dipped in very hot water and repeating the treatment several times. This was to prevent the bruise from swelling. Also to prevent the bruise swelling, a cloth could be folded five or six times, dipped in very cold water and applied to the bruise. When the cloth ceased to be cold it was to be removed and the process repeated.

Olive oil was the basis of another cure. A piece of cloth or wool was dipped in it and the bruise rubbed with it. The bruise was then covered with a compress saturated in oil.

Alternatively, a tallow candle was used. The bruise was rubbed with the cold tallow candle to prevent discoloration occurring.

A mixture of chopped parsley mixed with butter could also be applied, as could a piece of brown paper with treacle spread on it. A mixture of feverfew, ribwort, plantain, sage and bugle crushed and boiled in unsalted butter or vegetable oil was another suggested cure. This was strained and applied to the bruise.

A poultice could be made of hyssop leaves and applied to the bruise, and poultices could also be made from cabbage leaves or burdock. Mallow leaves crushed and mixed with unsalted butter or vegetable oil were advocated to be smeared on bruises to stop the pain and reduce the swelling.

A lotion could be made from infusing a handful of rosemary leaves in a pint of boiling water and adding the white of an egg and a teaspoon of brandy to the mixture when it was cool. Another lotion could be made from boiling some comfrey leaves.

The crushed fresh leaves of plantain were also thought to relieve bruising when applied to the bruised area, and yarrow and hops were both used externally. Rose water was thought to reduce swelling, as was lavender oil, while a poultice or compress of witch hazel was thought to be particularly effective in the treatment of bruises. Wintergreen, tansy and white horehound were thought to be useful in the treatment of bruises, as were celery, herb robert, fenugreek and hyssop.

bryony *see* **white bryony**.

buckthorn
The bark of buckthorn alder was used as a treatment for chronic constipation and piles.

Buckthorn is less common in Britain than buckthorn alder is. It too was used as a purgative and was also used as a diuretic. Externally it was used to treat bruises.

bugle
Bugle was used to stem the flow of blood from cuts and to stop the flow of menstrual blood. It was also used in heart disorders and in the relief of bronchitis.

bugloss, vipers
Bugloss was used in respiratory disorders to help bring up phlegm. It was also used as a diuretic. Feverish diseases were treated with it, as was inflammation. It was used in the relief of nervous complaints.

bunions
Belladonna and glycerine, painted on the affected area, was one cure. Later, iodine was used.

burdock

Burdock is a plant that was used in the treatment of boils, eczema and other skin complaints. It was also used to relieve bruising and burns.

Arthritis and rheumatism were said to be relieved by it, as was neuralgia. It was also used in the treatment of asthma and bronchitis and in the relief of indigestion.

burnet

Burnet is a plant that was used as a tonic and in heart disease. It was also used for stopping the menstrual flow. When applied externally it helped to speed up the healing process of wounds and running sores.

burns and scalds

Nowadays it is advocated that a burned area where possible should be put under cold running water and kept there for a considerable time. Alternatively, the burned area should be immersed in cold water.

In folk medicine there were several cures. Honey was thought to be an effective cure, and grated potato was also recommended. Egg white beaten until stiff and spread on the area of the burn was also thought to do good. An application of cold tea was another old remedy.

Grated raw carrot in a poultice was thought to be curative, as was onion juice and a lotion made from leeks cooked in milk. The crushed fresh leaves of plantain applied to the area were considered to speed healing, as were fresh nettle leaves and crushed dock leaves. Sage tea and an ointment made from comfrey were both thought to be curative.

Marigold, elderflowers and yarrow were all used as remedies for burns, and lavender was held to be particularly useful in minimizing scarring caused by burns. Witch hazel, eucalyptus and glycerine were all used to soothe burns.

One folk cure was based on pulverized charcoal and linseed oil. Another cure involved treating the area of the burn with a soft soap and linseed oil and then sprinkling wheaten flour over it to form a coating. A cloth saturated with linseed oil and lime water and bound round the burn was a suggested remedy for burns.

Chalk and linseed oil mixed to a thick compound was thought to be curative. Fern leaves were the basis of another cure. These were to be boiled with two pints of cream or vegetable fat and allowed to simmer. The mixture was cooled, strained and applied to the burn.

A lotion made from yellow dock, dandelion, plantain and greater celandine was held to be curative for burns. Another remedy suggested applying cream at once, while another advocated carbonate of soda.

There was certainly no shortage of suggested help for those unfortunate enough to burn themselves.

burr marigold

The plant was used to relieve gout and dropsy and to bring down fever. It was used in the treatment of haemorrhages and internal bleeding.

butterbur

Butterbur is also known as bog rhubarb. In early times it was used to bring down fever and promote perspiration.

C

cabbage

In ancient Rome cabbage was thought of as being a sovereign remedy that was useful for most things.

In folk medicine it was used as a tonic and in the treatment of stomach disorders, as well as for purifying the blood and cleansing the system. It was thought to have diuretic properties and was used in the treatment of arthritis.

Ulcers were thought to be healed by it, as was heartburn. It was considered to have antiseptic properties and was used to protect against respiratory infections.

In early times raw cabbage was taken to cure nervous complaints. It was also used in some liver conditions and was used to treat alcoholics and as a hangover cure.

Externally, cabbage was used to soothe, cleanse and heal the skin. It was used in the treatment of stings, burns, blisters, ulcers and sores. In the form of poultices, cabbage was used to bring boils to a head, to soothe chest infections and to bring relief to inflamed joints.

camomile *see* **chamomile**.

carrots

In folk medicine carrots were used from very early times
and for various conditions. They were traditionally considered to be aids to sharp eyesight and were thought to
be helpful in regulating the circulation. They were also
thought to regulate the menstrual cycle and increase the
flow of milk in nursing mothers.

Carrots were also taken in the belief that they would
act as an appetite stimulant and be effective in a number
of disorders associated with the digestive system. They
were used to treat flatulence, colic, ulcers, constipation,
diarrhoea and haemorrhoids.

They were thought to be diuretic and were used in the
treatment of cystitis, gout and arthritis. They were also
thought to be expectorant and were used in various respiratory disorders.

Externally carrots were used, sometimes in a poultice, to speed up the healing of wounds, ulcers, boils
and styes. They were also used to treat eczema and chilblains.

castor oil

Castor oil is one of the oldest remedies known, and it
has been used as a laxative for thousands of years. It has
a particularly unpleasant odour and taste and so was

difficult to take. One old remedy suggests floating it on hot milk and eating a piece of orange or lemon peel before taking it. Alternatively, something with a strong taste, such as peppermint, could be taken before, with, or after it.

External castor oil was used as a hair conditioner and as a remedy for dandruff and hair fall. It was also thought to be effective in treating eye irritation caused by the presence of a foreign body in the eye.

catarrh

Honey taken with tea was an old remedy for catarrh, as was a mixture of cinnamon and lemon juice taken in warm water. An infusion of elderflowers, peppermint and yarrow was also thought to be effective.

A mixture of herbs taken in the form of a tea was thought to be useful in the treatment of catarrh. The herbs involved were coltsfoot, mullein, thyme and yarrow.

Another cure involved heating a pint of milk with mace, nutmeg, cinnamon and sugar until it was on the point of boiling. Two glasses of white wine or sherry were then added and the mixture heated and stirred until it curdled. It was then strained and given to the patient.

A snuff made from a mixture of roasted coffee, menthol and sugar ground together to make a powder was another suggested old remedy.

It was often thought that the bowels were involved in a whole range of illnesses, and aperients were recommended in catarrh.

Cinnamon, ginger, cloves, chamomile, rosemary, sage, thyme, rose, lavender, borage and balm were used in the treatment of catarrh, as were pepper, tea, vinegar, witch hazel and olive oil. Onions, leeks and garlic were thought to be effective catarrh remedies, as were watercress, turnip juice, elder, plantain, yarrow, marigold, myrrh and nettle. Eucalyptus was a common remedy.

catnip

Catnip is also known as catmint. Cats are attracted to it because of its distinctive smell.

In folk medicine it was used as a remedy for colic and flatulence and also to treat stomach upsets and diarrhoea.

Catnip was also used to treat bronchitis, colds and influenza. Anaemia was also treated with it, and it was used to induce the menstrual flow.

It was thought to be useful in treating nervous conditions and insomnia.

Externally it was used to treat cuts, bruises and sores.

celery

Celery is also known as wild celery or common celery.

It was thought to be a diuretic and was used in the treatment of gout, arthritis and rheumatism. It was thought to be an appetite stimulant and to cure flatulence.

Celery was taken as a tonic and used to raise the mood in cases of depression. It was also used to treat nervous disorders and was considered to be a remedy for hysteria and insomnia. It was thought to have aphrodisiac powers.

centaury
Centaury was used as an aid to digestion and as a stimulant of the appetite. It was used as a remedy for indigestion and as a tonic. Nervous disorders were treated with it.

chamomile

chamomile
Chamomile is frequently spelt camomile.

The early herbalists used it to cure cases of fluid

62

retention and jaundice. It was also used to treat menstrual pain, painful joints and asthma. It was thought to reduce fevers, cure insomnia and stimulate the appetite.

It was used as sedative in nervous disorders. Externally, it was used to soothe rashes and bruises, to heal sores and to reduce inflammation.

chervil

Chervil was used in folk medicine to purify the blood. High blood pressure was treated with it, and it was used as a remedy for gallstones and bronchitis. It was also used as a diuretic and as an aid to digestion.

Externally, it was used to treat skin disorders, abscesses and sores.

chickweed

Chickweed is also known as adder's mouth and starwort.

In folk medicine it was used as an expectorant in the treatment of bronchitis. It was also used as a laxative and as a cure for rheumatism and arthritis. Period pains were treated with it, and it was used externally to treat skin diseases, wounds, bruises, burns and abrasions.

chilblains

Old remedies for chilblains included angelica, garlic, glycerine, hawthorn, horseradish and mugwort. Onion, shepherd's purse and watercress were also used. Other cures included slices of raw potato, a lotion made from raw carrot, turnip poultices, crushed fresh marigold flowers applied to the chilblains or mustard taken internally.

An old cure for unbroken chilblains involved applying a lotion made from linseed oil, oil of turpentine and spirits of camphor. Another was made from oil of lavender, liquid carbolic acid and oxide of zinc ointment.

childbirth
Several courses of action were recommended well in advance of the actual labour to ease childbirth. One old piece of advice was that raspberry tea should be taken when women were about six months pregnant. This was thought to prevent miscarriage and increase the milk supply. Another suggestion was that pregnant women during pregnancy should take linseed tea with added honey.

During labour clove oil was sometimes used as a massage oil to increase the strength of the contractions. Marigold was also thought to strengthen contractions, as was myrrh. Parsley was thought to be helpful to get the uterus back to normal after childbirth, although, since it was thought to stimulate the muscles of the uterus, pregnant women were advised to avoid it during pregnancy. Chamomile was used as a relaxant during childbirth.

cinnamon

Cinnamon was used to stimulate the circulation and in the treatment of colds, catarrh and respiratory infections, especially when there was fever present. It was also used as a remedy for disorders of the digestive system and was used in diarrhoea, flatulence, colic and nausea.

It was also thought to stop heavy bleeding, and it was used in nosebleeds and in heavy menstrual bleeding. Muscle pains and arthritis were also treated by it.

Externally, it was used as an antiseptic for the relief of wounds, abrasions and stings and in skin conditions. Cinnamon was also used to treat head lice.

cinquefoil

Cinquefoil is also known as wild tansy, silverweed and gooseweed.

It was used as an antispasmodic to relieve muscular spasm and spasms of the uterus. Stomach pains and painful menstruation were also thought to be relieved by it. Early herbalists used it to treat epilepsy.

It was used as a gargle for sore throats and as a mouthwash for mouth ulcers. Externally it was used in the treatment of abrasions and wounds.

cloves

Cloves were particularly used for the relief of toothache because of the numbing effect that cloves can produce. It was used as an aid to digestion and as a cure for indigestion and to relieve nausea.

They were used in the treatment of nervous disorders, such as excessive anxiety, and also in the treatment of depression. They were thought to have expectorant properties and were used in the treatment of colds and other respiratory infections.

Cloves were also thought to be able to induce perspiration and bring down fevers. They were also thought to relieve hay fever. Diarrhoea and flatulence were both treated with cloves.

Oil of cloves was used as a massage oil to strengthen uterine contractions in childbirth. Rubbed on the temples it was thought to be a remedy for headaches. Cuts, wounds and ringworm were treated with it, and it was used as a liniment for aching joints.

colds

A syrup made from coltsfoot was an old cure for colds, as was an infusion of peppermint leaves with added honey. A tea made from dried yarrow leaves and dried elderflowers was recommended before retiring at night as a cold cure. Barley water was another cold cure.

Another old cure for colds involved mixing yarrow, ginger root, cayenne pepper and water and boiling these together with the addition of honey. Alternatively, fresh elderflowers and angelica leaves could be soaked in boiling water and strained. The resulting liquid was used, sweetened with honey, for the relief of colds.

Elderberries formed the basis of another cure. These were simmered with brown sugar until the mixture was the consistency of honey before being administered in hot water.

Rubbing the chest with oil of rosemary was thought to bring relief to those suffering from colds. Wringing out a piece of flannel in boiling water, sprinkling it with turpentine and placing it on the chest was also thought to help. A more curious remedy was the rubbing of the soles of the feet with a mixture of crushed garlic bulbs and white horehound.

Hot mustard foot-baths, inhalations of eucalyptus in boiling water and drinking hot lemonade were all popular cold remedies.

See also COUGHS; RESPIRATORY INFECTIONS.

colic

An old cure for colic involved administering a drink made from betony boiled in white wine.

Parsley, peppermint, chamomile, cinnamon, sage, thyme and meadowsweet were all used in the treatment of colic. The juice of raw potato, cabbage, carrot were considered to be remedies, as was glycerine.

coltsfoot

Coltsfoot was mainly used in the treatment of colds, coughs, bronchial disorders and asthma.

Externally it was used in the form of poultices to treat sores and burns.

comfrey

comfrey

Comfrey is a plant also known as knitbone.

Comfrey was primarily used as an aid to the healing of fractured bones. It was also known as a cough remedy and was used in the treatment of asthma and tuberculosis. Dysentery was also treated with it, and it was used in the treatment of anaemia and as a tonic for invalids.

It was used as a gargle for sore throats, and externally the leaves were used in a poultice for the relief of abrasions, wounds, bruises and varicose veins. It was also used externally to ease painful joints.

constipation *see* laxative.

corns
Marigold used externally in the form of an infusion or in the form of crushed flowers was an old remedy for corns. Corns were also treated with castor oil to soften them and make them easier to remove.

Celandine juice applied to the corn and left to dry was thought to be effective. A mixture of apple juice, carrot juice and salt was also considered to relieve corns, as were crushed ivy leaves applied daily.

consumption *see* tuberculosis.

coughs
Honey and lemon were used in the treatment of coughs, as were garlic, onions, leeks and olive oil. Cabbage, carrots and turnips were also used, as were comfrey, nettle, dock, rosemary, lavender, thyme, balm, linseed,

glycerine and peppermint. Eucalyptus was a common cure.

There were many old cures for coughs. One of these involved making a hole through a lemon and filling it with honey. The lemon was then roasted and the juice collected and given to the patient. Another involved cutting a hole through a swede and filling the hole with brown sugar. This was left overnight and the juice given to the patient.

Many herbal drinks were recommended. An infusion of coltsfoot leaves sweetened with honey was recommended, as was a syrup made from boiling coltsfoot leaves and an equal amount of plantain leaves with an equal amount of honey. In another remedy involving coltsfoot leaves, they were boiled with garlic in water and had brown sugar added.

Dried sage, vinegar and honey formed the basis of another remedial drink, as did dried sage, ginger, brown sugar and water. Butter, honey and vinegar were mixed and heated to form another cure, and hyssop, hartshorn, almond oil, sugar and water were mixed to make yet another. An infusion of horehound, marshmallow leaves, hyssop, mullein and ground coriander was also used.

A less readily available cure involved mixing the juice of leeks with the breast milk of a nursing mother. A distinctly less acceptable old cure involved the boiling of two or three snails in barley water.

See also BRONCHITIS; EXPECTORANTS; RESPIRATORY INFECTIONS.

cowslip
Cowslip was used by early herbalists as a remedy for palsy. It was also used as a sedative in various nervous disorders and as a cure for insomnia. The plant was used as a remedy for spasm and as an expectorant.

Cowslip had to be used with caution as it had irritant properties and could result in allergic reactions.

cowslip

cramps *see* **abdominal pains** *and* **menstruation**.

cucumber

Cucumber was used in folk medicine to reduce heat and inflammation in various infections, such as lung and chest conditions and skin conditions. It was also used to bring down fevers.

It was thought to be a mild diuretic and to be able to cleanse the system. Gout and arthritis were treated with it, as was eczema.

Externally cucumber was used to soothe inflamed skin and to soothe irritated eyes. It was also used on sunburn and was used cosmetically in the belief that it would keep the skin young and wrinkle-free.

cuts *see* **abrasions**.

D

dandelion

The leaves and root of the dandelion were used in traditional herbal medicine. Dandelion was known principally as a diuretic, being used in cases of fluid retention.

It was also used as a mild laxative, as a tonic and as a stimulant of the appetite and aid to the digestion. Gout, rheumatism, arthritis, indigestion, jaundice, hepatitis, gall-bladder infections and congestion of the chest were also thought to be relieved by dandelion.

Dandelion was also used in cases of insomnia. Anaemia and circulatory disorders were also treated by it, as were diabetes, headaches, fatigue and irritability.

As a cure for warts the juice of the dandelion was applied to the affected areas. An infusion of the leaves and flowers was used as a wash for some skin complaints.

dandruff

Sulphur was used in the treatment of dandruff. One ounce of sulphur and two pints of water were shaken together repeatedly every few hours and then the head was soaked with the liquid. Alternatively, an ointment of weak sulphur and lanolin was used.

Yarrow used as a rinse was regarded as being a cure for dandruff as well as being thought to prevent hair falling out. Castor oil rubbed into the scalp was also supposed to have both of these effects, while a shampoo made from nettle was meant to cure the dandruff.

An infusion of sage brushed into the scalp every night was thought to be effective, and it was also thought to improve the condition of the hair generally. Another later cure was a mixture of kerosene and water, equal parts being used. For the first few days of treatment this was to be rubbed into the hair night and morning.

See also HAIR.

debility

In cases of debility, such as that which occurs after a long illness, several remedies were suggested. These included the use of oats, wheat, milk, cinnamon and cayenne.

Cabbage and turnip were thought to be instrumental in building up people's strength. Nettle and dock were also used, as were rosemary, yarrow, lavender and witch hazel.

diabetes

Natural substances that lowered blood sugar and so was

used in the treatment of diabetes included oats. Apples were also thought to help regulate blood sugar.

Cabbage was also thought to assist the reduction of blood sugar, as were onions. Dandelion and burdock were also said to be beneficial in the relief of diabetes.

diarrhoea

Honey, cinnamon, ginger, lemon, apple, egg, tea, barley, cloves, garlic, leeks and carrot were thought to be able to relieve diarrhoea. Chamomile, sage, rose-hips, nettle, dock, marigold, thyme, yarrow, hawthorn, meadowsweet, peppermint, witch hazel and eucalyptus leaves were also used in the treatment of the condition.

Agrimony, avens, herb robert, marjoram, sage, slippery elm and sorrel were also thought to have properties that would cure diarrhoea. Tea made from raspberry leaves was thought to be an effective cure. A mixture of flour was also recommended for the condition.

depression

In folk medicine depression was treated by oats. Other remedies included mustard, cloves, rosemary, cardamom, rose, dock, yarrow, thyme, lavender and balm.

digestion, aid to

There were various natural substances that were thought to be aids to digestion. These included ginger, cinnamon, peppermint, pepper, mustard, apple and barley. Other aids to digestion were garlic, onion, parsley and cardamom, chamomile, dandelion, burdock, nettle, sage, thyme, rosemary, yarrow and lavender.

Lemon balm, hawthorn, eucalyptus and myrrh have also been used to aid and stimulate the digestion.

digestive problems

Lemon, although it is generally regarded as an acid, was thought to be helpful in some digestive problems. The juice of raw potato was also used, as were ginger and cider vinegar.

An old folk remedy involved the use of white mustard. Another was based on oats.

Peppermint has been used in connection with digestive disorders for a long time. Olive oil, chamomile, marigold, balm and meadowsweet were also thought to be effective.

dill

We now know dill mainly as a culinary herb, but it was also used in medicine. In early times it was regarded as an aphrodisiac and was an ingredient in love potions.

Dill was used as a cure for flatulence, colic and indigestion. It was also found to be effective as a stimulant of the appetite and to promote the milk flow in nursing mothers.

People used to chew dill seeds to sweeten the breath and cure halitosis.

diphtheria

An old remedy suggested that if you thought that you were at risk from diphtheria you should gargle the throat immediately with lemon juice. Lavender was given to try to alleviate the disease as it has antiseptic and anti-bacterial properties. Yellow dock was also used.

diuretics

Diuretics are substances that promote the flow of urine and cure fluid retention. Many natural substances were thought to have diuretic properties. These include watercress, lemon, wheat, leeks, carrots, onions, turnip and cucumber. Dandelion, parsley, plantain, burdock, nettle, garlic and yellow dock were also considered to be natural diuretics.

Practitioners of folk medicine had no shortage of plants that were held to have diuretic properties. As well as those above, they could choose from rosemary, rose, marigold and yarrow. Lavender, juniper, thyme, hawthorn, borage, elder and meadowsweet were also regarded as natural diuretics, some being stronger in their effect than others.

Other natural diuretics include agrimony, arnica, asparagus, bearberry, belladonna, bilberry, bittersweet,

dizziness

blackcurrant, boneset, buckthorn, burdock, burr marigold, catmint, chervil, golden rod, groundsel, heartsease,
hyssop, kidneywort, lily of the valley, madder, wild lettuce, marjoram, white poppy, sorrel, speedwell, ragwort,
holy thistle, vervain and yarrow.

dizziness

Thyme was a traditional remedy for dizziness or vertigo.
Hawthorn was another traditional cure, and balm and
fenugreek were also thought to relieve the condition.

People suffering from frequent dizzy spells were advised to drink sage tea sweetened with honey. Alternatively, a drink could be taken made from cowslips boiled
in water, with honey added to taste.

dock

Broad-leaved dock was used as a tonic and as a purgative. It was also used in jaundice and as a laxative. Broad-
leaved dock had to be used with care as it caused skin
allergy or nausea.

Dock was a well-known cure for nettle stings, and it
was used to treat ringworm and scabies.

dock, yellow

Yellow dock is also known as curled dock.

In traditional medicine it had several roles. It was used
as a mild laxative and as a cure for ulcers and bowel

infections. Gout, cystitis and jaundice were also treated
by it, and it was used as a diuretic.

Yellow dock was used to treat arthritis and rheumatism. Chronic skin disease was also thought to be cured
by it.

It was used to regulate the menstrual cycle and as a
tonic for people suffering from debility or recovering
from an illness. Dock seeds were a traditional cure for
dysentery, diarrhoea and haemorrhages.

dog rose

The fruit of the dog rose is a rich source of vitamin C
and was used to treat the common cold and influenza. It
was also used as a laxative, as a tonic and as a treatment
for disorders of the gall bladder.

dropsy

Parsley was an old cure for dropsy, as was the root of
the dock, both of these to be taken in the form of infusions. A mixture consisting of small quantities of foxglove and broom was recommended to be taken in the
form of a tea.

Another suggested cure involved bruising artichoke
leaves in a mortar, straining the resultant liquid and adding it to Madeira wine. This was to be taken every morning and evening.

Wine was also involved in another cure, but this time

it was white wine. The tops of green broom were dried in an oven and burnt to ashes on a clean hearth. The ashes were mixed with the wine and the mixture left to stand all night to allow it to settle. The clearest part of it was drunk in the morning, late afternoon and at night before retiring.

Any herbs with diuretic properties were also used in the treatment of dropsy, which was a disorder involving fluid retention. A tea made from the root of the elder was meant to be effective.

There were several old remedies that were to be applied externally. One of these involved crushing black snails with bay salt and applying the mixture to the soles of the feet. A more pleasant one involved the bruising of peppermint leaves and wormwood leaves and boiling them in cream until they formed an oil. This was then strained and smeared on any areas swollen with dropsy.

dysentery

An old country cure for dysentery was to make a drink from cinnamon powder stirred into milk. Another old cure was vinegar diluted with water, and yet another was pepper. Dock seeds were another traditional remedy.

A drink made from milk, nutmeg, peppercorns, cloves, cinnamon and oak bark was thought to bring relief to sufferers from dysentery.

Raw grated apple was thought to help in cases of dysentery, as was honey. Thyme, meadowsweet, witch hazel and the leaves of eucalyptus, too, were meant to be able to relieve the condition.

A cure to be applied externally used garlic. The garlic was pressed and heated until it was quite hot. A piece of cloth was folded and dipped in the garlic and then placed on the navel until it grew cold. The treatment could be repeated two or three times.

dyspepsia *see* **indigestion**.

E

earache

An old cure for earache involved putting a pinch of black pepper in a very small piece of cotton wadding or cotton wool. The wadding was then dipped in corn oil or some form of sweet oil and inserted into the ear. A flannel bandage was tied over the head to keep the ear warm.

Another cure suggested bathing the ears with a decoction of chamomile. Yet another, supposedly a very quick cure, involved the boiling of an onion until it was soft. The soft onion pulp was then rubbed on the inside of the ear.

Earache is a common and painful disease, and so it is no wonder that there were several folk cures. A mixture of green elder and leek juice was used in another cure. A branch of green elder was placed over a low fire. An egg-cup of sap was collected from the elder as it exuded from the wood and this was added to an egg-cup of leek juice. This was thoroughly mixed and applied to the affected ear three times a day.

In another folk cure, a mustard leaf was put just behind the ear, and in another baked apple was applied to the ear. Warmed honey or almond oil could be dripped into the ear to bring relief. Garlic oil or lavender oil in warmed olive oil was also used in this way, as was peppermint oil.

An infusion of plantain taken internally was thought to be curative in cases of earache.

Heat treatment was generally recommended. Originally, hot cloths were placed on the side of the head with the affected ear. Later hot-water bottles were used.

eczema

Eczema is a condition of the skin in which the skin becomes red and itchy and starts to flake and weep.

A tea made from marigold flowers was an old cure for eczema. Another internal cure was a drink made from hot water, lemon juice, honey and cayenne pepper, while yet another was a decoction of dock.

A cure applied externally involved boiling a handful of watercress in water, straining the mixture, allowing it to cool and then bathing the areas affected with eczema two or three times a day. Watercress was also taken internally to try and effect a cure.

A broth made from carrot was applied to affected areas to relieve itching from eczema. Olive oil was used to soothe skin affected by the condition, as was glycerine. Bathing with a little vinegar and water was also thought to soothe skin irritation.

Cucumber juice was also advocated as a soother of inflamed skin, and burdock poultices were sometimes applied to help heal the skin. Marigold used externally was also thought to help the healing process and reduce inflammation. Lemon balm was also applied externally to reduce inflammation.

A poultice was made from the leaves and flowers of borage to relieve eczema, while the root and bark of elder was made into an ointment to cure it.

egg

Eggs have long been regarded as being exceptionally nutritious. Nowadays we tend to eat fewer of them because they are high in cholesterol. In folk remedies, however, they were much valued as an easily digested food for invalids and convalescents to build up their strength.

Raw eggs or very lightly boiled eggs were used as a tonic. Stomach disorders were also treated with eggs in this way, eggs being thought to be helpful in cases of indigestion, constipation and diarrhoea.

Various light foods based on eggs, such as egg custard, were given to invalids. Drinks based on eggs were also given to invalids to give them more strength. These included eggnog, one recipe for which involved beating a egg yolk with milk and then adding some brandy and a beaten egg white. A small amount of lime water was thought to make this more digestible.

Egg white, beaten up in milk, was taken as an antidote to some corrosive poisons.

Eggs were also used externally to soothe the skin. The white of eggs was applied in layers, time being given for each layer to dry, to cracked nipples in nursing mothers, to babies' bottoms affected by nappy rash and to the skin of people affected by sunburn.

One cure for burns involved eggs. The whites of eggs were beaten until stiff and spread over the burn.

Another use for eggs was to prevent hair from falling out. In this remedy eggs were beaten, mixed with water and rubbed into the scalp. This was left on overnight and washed out the next morning.

Eggs were also used to shampoo the hair to improve its general condition.

elder

Common names for elder include black elder, bore tree and bour tree. The bark, leaves, flowers and berries were all used in herbal medicine, making it a very versatile remedy that has been in use for many hundreds of years.

An old superstition had it that if you gathered elder branches on May Day pieces of the branches could be used to cure the bite of a rabid dog. Another superstition claimed that if you carried a twig of elder in your pocket it would protect you against rheumatism.

The bark of the elder was used as a strong purgative and, if taken in large doses, was an emetic. A tincture from the bark was used to relieve the symptoms of asthma and croup, and the bark has also been used in epilepsy.

The leaves were used as a purgative and a diuretic. They were helpful in conditions requiring an expectorant or one in which perspiration was required to be induced.

Elder leaves were used externally to cure sprains, bruises, chilblains, open wounds and piles. They were used to relieve headaches by placing them on the temples.

The root of the elder was curative in some respects. A tea was made from it as a cure for dropsy. It was also used in an ointment for eczema and psoriasis and in a decoction used as a mouthwash.

The flowers of the elder are mildly astringent and were used in eye lotions and skin lotions. The dried flowers were used to make a tea that had a laxative effect and was also used to induce perspiration. Taken before going to sleep, a hot elderflower infusion was considered to be a cure for colds, laryngitis, tonsillitis, sinus trouble and influenza, having decongestant and expectorant properties.

It was supposed to have a relaxant effect and was

thought to be a cure for the spasms caused by asthma. Taken before breakfast, it was meant to purify the blood. A hot infusion of elderflowers was also given in cases of eruptive diseases, such as measles and chickenpox, supposedly to bring out the rash and aid recovery.

Elderflowers were thought to be diuretic and were used to relieve fluid retention. They were used in the treatment of gout and arthritis.

The flowers of the elder were used in poultices, ointments or lotions to reduce inflammation, to heal wounds and to bring relief to burns and scalds. The same treatment was used to relieve chapped hands and chilblains.

The berries, as well as being used to make wine, were used to treat coughs and colds. They also had laxative properties. Taken internally, elderberries were used as a remedy for neuralgia and sciatica. Medieval herbalists used them to bring on menstruation.

elecampane

The flowering plant elecampane has the common name of elfwort.

Its main use in folk medicine was as an expectorant in the treatment of bronchial coughs. Elecampane was also used in the relief of fluid retention and as an antiseptic.

It was thought to induce menstruation. Invalids were

thought to find it useful as it was used as a tonic and a stimulant of the appetite.

elm

The dried inner bark of the elm, also called field elm or broad-leaved elm, had various uses in folk medicine.

It was used as a diuretic and a tonic. Scurvy and other skin diseases were thought to be improved by a decoction of it.

Used in a poultice, it was thought to reduce the pain caused by gout or rheumatism.

elm

emetic

An emetic is something that induces vomiting.

One common emetic used in cases of poisoning or in cases where too much indigestible food had been eaten consisted of a teaspoonful of English mustard in a glass of warm water. Salt and water was also used. An older emetic was a mixture of salt and vinegar.

Some herbs and plants are natural emetics. These include adder's tongue, elder black mustard, thistle (holy) and vervain.

Ipecacuanha wine was administered as an emetic also, especially to children.

epilepsy

Epilepsy is a condition in which sufferers are subject to sudden fits.

The early herbalists regarded lavender as being a remedy for epilepsy. Arab herbalists used balm in the treatment of the disease. Later, foxglove was thought to bring relief.

There was a curious treatment for epilepsy. This involved the patient creeping, head foremost, down three pairs of stairs three times a day for three days in a row.

Epilepsy was once thought to be caused by witchcraft. A cure reflecting this fact involved filling a quart bottle with pins and placing the bottle in front of the

fire until the pins were red hot. The idea behind this
practice was that the heart of the supposed witch behind the epilepsy would be pricked by the hot pins. She
would then be in such agony that she would stop inflict-
ing epilepsy on her victim.

Because of its supposed connection with witchcraft,
charms were once carried to ward off epilepsy. A very
popular charm was a ring made from a piece of silver
collected from the offering made in church by the con-
gregation.

Epsom salts

Epsom salts, also known as magnesium sulphate, are
colourless, odourless crystals that taste very bitter.

Taken with a little water by mouth, they are used as a
quick-acting purgative in cases of chronic constipation.
They are also used as a remedy for indigestion, biliousness and fluid retention.

Bathing in water with Epsom salts added was regarded
as being beneficial in cases of gout and arthritis.

eucalyptus

The eucalyptus tree is also known as the fever tree.

Because of its antiseptic, disinfectant properties, it was
planted in areas of swamp to purify those areas that were
breeding grounds for fevers and other diseases.

An inhalation of a few drops of eucalyptus oil was

used for the relief of cold symptoms. It was also used as an expectorant in asthma, bronchitis and pneumonia and as a decongestant in catarrh and sinusitis.

A decoction of the leaves was used for the relief of dysentery, typhoid, diarrhoea, and vomiting. Disorders of the urinary tract, such as cystitis, were also treated with a decoction of eucalyptus leaves.

Eucalyptus taken internally was also thought to stimulate the circulation, induce sweating, reduce fever and speed up eruptive diseases, such as chickenpox, by bringing out the eruptions on to the skin.

Externally eucalyptus oil was used in compresses to be applied to wounds, burns, ulcers, boils and abscesses as an antiseptic and either to stop bleeding or to speed up healing. Some drops of eucalyptus oil in almond oil was used to rub the chest in chest infections, bronchitis and asthma. Ringworm and athlete's foot were treated with dilute eucalyptus, and this was also used as an application to the skin as an insect repellent.

expectorants

An expectorant is something that helps to remove the secretions from the bronchi, lungs and trachea. When people have taken an expectorant, they usually cough up phlegm.

Herbs that were thought to be natural expectorants include boneset, bugloss, coltsfoot, comfrey, elder, fennel, fenugreek, garlic, honeysuckle, hyssop, Jacob's ladder, larch, white poppy, St John's wort, sundew and violet.

sundew was thought to be a natural expectorant

eyebright

Eyebright is a plant also known as meadow eyebright and euphrasia.

It is usually used in the form of an infusion in water or milk, but it can be used in a lotion or ointment or in the form of expressed juice.

As its name suggests, eyebright was most commonly used for weak eyesight or other disorders of the eye. It was also used in the treatment of catarrh, sinusitis and inflammation.

Early herbalists also used it to restore a poor memory and in cases of dizziness.

eye problems

An old cure for sore eyes was the application of a poultice made of raw grated apple to the eyes. Cucumber juice applied to the eyes was a common cure for sore eyes and one that is still frequently used in home beauty treatments, as is witch hazel, which was also a common old cure for bathing sore eyes.

An infusion of plantain was applied to sore eyelids, and this was also used as an eyewash for sore eyes. A decoction of comfrey root or an infusion of the comfrey leaves was used as an eyewash for inflamed eyes. Rose water was also used to soothe sore eyes, as was an eyewash made from dock and one made from yarrow.

Itching eyes were thought to be cured by applying a liquid distilled from meadowsweet, according to an old remedy. An oil made from balm reduced inflammation of the eyes. Castor oil also soothed irritated eyes, especially when the irritation was caused by the presence of a foreign body.

Styes in the eye were thought to be relieved by the application of a teaspoon of a poultice made from tea, according to another old remedy. It was also suggested that they be bathed frequently with warm milk and water or with warm poppy water. Yet another old cure advocated the taking of a dose of Epsom salts with a squeeze of lemon in it as a purgative to cure styes. Since styes were thought to be a sign of poor general health, quinine and iron tonics were advised.

Swollen eyelids were thought to be alleviated by the application of grated potato mixed in a little olive oil.

Discoloration around the eye was said to be helped by scraping the fresh root of Solomon's seal, moistening it with vinegar and applying the mixture to the area round the eye.

Herbs not already mentioned but thought to be effective in disorders of the eye included angelica, betony, borage, catnip, cowslip, feverfew, lilac, lovage, poppy, sage, viper's bugloss and white horehound.

eyesight

Carrots were said to improve the eyesight, as was eyebright. Rosemary was also used to cure weak eyesight by early herbalists, as was lavender.

A suggested treatment for weak eyes involved the spraying of a jet of weak salt water on the eyelid. Another recommended bathing the eyes with cold tea or cold water to which a little Epsom salts has been added.

It was suggested that men with poor eyesight should abstain from sexual intercourse to improve their sight. An old suggested cure for blindness was to make a poultice from the leaves of celery. If the blindness affected only one eye, say the right one, the poultice was to be placed on the other wrist, in the suggested case the left wrist. In cases where both eyes were affected poultices were to be placed on both wrists.

eyestrain

In cases of eyestrain in which the eyes were puffy the sufferer was advised to apply a raw potato to the eye to reduce the swelling.

Tired eyes could be helped by an infusion of elderflowers in water. When cool, this was used to bathe the eyes. Alternatively, an infusion of raspberry leaves, marshmallow leaves and groundsel leaves could be used as an eyewash.

A rather messy cure consisted of butter or vegetable fat blended with honey and the white of an egg. The affected eye was to be smeared with this mixture. A cure for eyestrain whose ingredients might be difficult to find involved the use of the breast milk of two different nursing mothers. This was to be applied to the eyes.

F

fainting

Rosemary and lavender were used as a cure for fainting, and peppermint was used as an inhalant during fainting fits.

fat hen

Fat hen is a plant also known as pigweed or white goosefeet, and it is related to spinach. It is rich in iron and was used in folk medicine to cure anaemia. It was also used as a laxative.

Fat hen was usually administered in the form of an infusion of the dried herb.

fennel

Fennel is also known as sweet fennel and wild fennel. It is now chiefly known as a vegetable and culinary herb but the seeds, leaves and roots were also used in herbal medicine.

In ancient Greece, fennel was thought to increase the

fennel

flow of milk in nursing mothers. In old folklore, fennel was thought to increase the libido and cure impotence and frigidity. For this reason it was used in love potions.

Later, fennel was used as a cure for flatulence, colic and indigestion. It had various other uses, including being a cure for obesity.

It was used as a diuretic and was thought to be helpful in the cure of jaundice and disorders of the gall bladder. However, children suffering from bed-wetting were also thought to be helped by the herb.

Toothache and earache were meant to be cured by fennel, and it was used as an expectorant in bronchitis.

fenugreek

Fennel had to be used with caution as an overdose could affect the nervous system and fresh fennel leaves could be an irritant.

fenugreek

Early herbalists thought that the bruised leaves of fenugreek placed on the head cured dizziness. In the seventeenth century, women who had just given birth were advised to sit with their legs open over the fumes coming from a decoction of fenugreek to help to expel the placenta.

Later it was used as an expectorant in bronchitis. It was also used as a tonic and in a gargle for sore throats.

Externally it was applied to treat wounds, sores and boils.

fertility

Watercress was thought to be an aid to fertility. Ginger was thought to be a cure for impotence, and oats were meant to be a cure for sterility and impotence. Wheat was considered to promote fertility, as was rose.

The ancient Romans used sage as a cure for infertility.

fever

Substances that reduce fever are known as febrifuges. In herbal medicine these included aconite, avens, balm, blackcurrant, bogbean and boneset.

Also used in feverish illnesses were angelica, betony,

borage, catnip and cowslip. Feverfew, lilac, and meadow-sweet were also recommended treatments, as were poppy, sage, white horehound and yarrow.

Cinnamon, watercress, honey, vinegar, pepper, lemon and apple were used to help cure feverish illnesses. Cloves, parsley, plantain and chamomile also played a part, as did burdock, nettle, rosemary, rose, marigold, yarrow, lavender, balm, hawthorn, meadowsweet, peppermint and eucalyptus.

feverfew

The old herbalists used feverfew to help expel the placenta after childbirth and in cases of stillbirth.

Feverfew was used as a laxative and as a sedative. It was also used to encourage the menstrual flow.

Coughs and wheezing were treated with it, as were colic, flatulence and indigestion. Feverfew was also used in the treatment of headaches and in nervous complaints. It was recommended as a tonic and as a raiser of the spirits.

Earache and insect and vermin bites were thought to be eased by the application of feverfew.

figwort

Figwort is also known as heal-all.

Early herbalists used it to cure the skin disease scrofula. Later, it was used as a diuretic and as a mild laxative. It was also used as a stimulant in heart disease.

Externally figwort was used in the treatment of skin diseases and to help reduce the swelling of bruises.

It was usually administered in the form of an infusion of the dried root stock or of the flowers.

flatulence

Peppermint, cinnamon and ginger were thought to be useful in the treatment of flatulence, as were cloves and barley. Carrots, onions, parsley, nettle, dock, chamomile and cardamon were also thought to be effective cures.

Thyme, lavender, myrrh, olive oil and eucalyptus were also known as remedies for flatulence. Angelica, caraway, catnip, celery, coriander, dill, fennel, feverfew, horseradish, tansy and woodruff were used also.

flax

Another name for flax is linseed.

The seeds and oil expressed from the seeds were used in herbal medicine.

It was used in the treatment of bronchitis and disorders of the lungs, being also an ingredient of some cough mixtures. Constipation was also relieved by it.

A poultice of the seeds, sometimes in conjunction with mustard, was used externally in the treatment of boils, abscesses, ulcers and areas of inflammation. When mixed with lime water, linseed oil was used on burns and scalds.

flax

fluid retention *see* **diuretics**.

food poisoning
Early herbalists used garlic in cases of food poisoning. Castor oil was also used to cure this.

foxglove

The leaves of the foxglove were used in heart disease, increasing the activity of the heart muscles.

The foxglove was used as a diuretic in dropsy, and it was also used in kidney disease. It was also used in the treatment of epilepsy, in inflammatory diseases and in delirium tremens. Internal haemorrhaging was also treated by it.

Care had to be taken with foxglove because it could have poisonous effects.

fractures *see* **bones, broken**.

freckles

Freckles were thought to be removed by the application of the crushed leaves or juice of watercress.

A paste that was meant to remove freckles was made from sour milk and horseradish. This was applied with a brush.

Another method that was supposed to remove freckles involved making a mixture of fresh cream, milk, lemon juice, brandy, sugar and eau de Cologne, boiling the mixture, skimming it and applying it to the freckled area.

Yet another method consisted of combining muriate of ammonia with lavender water and distilled water. A rather complicated method involved dipping a bunch of grapes in a basin of water. These were then sprinkled with a mixture of powdered alum and salt, the grapes wrapped in paper and baked. The juice was squeezed out and applied to the face. This preparation was also thought to be able to remove a tan.

A mixture of lemon and glycerine was meant to make freckles less obvious.

fumitory

This is a plant that early herbalists thought could improve the eyesight, and in the Middle Ages young women used it to wash themselves to make skin blemishes disappear.

Later it was used as a laxative and as a diuretic. It was also used to treat conjunctivitis and serious skin diseases.

Fumitory was extremely toxic, and it was recommended for use only by someone skilled in herbal medicine.

G

gall bladder problems

Several plants were thought to have a beneficial effect on the gall bladder. These included betony, marigold, peony, pimpernel and vervain. Dandelion and yarrow were also thought to be helpful, as were apples and olive oil.

Barberry, chicory, dandelion root, knotgrass and peppermint were thought to be effective treatments for gallstones. Potatoes and lemons were also considered to be curative.

garlic

Garlic is a very old remedy, it being known from early times for its power to cure infections. It was the bulb of the plant that was used. Nowadays we know it mostly as a culinary ingredient, although many people take garlic pills as a health supplement.

It was used in very many ways. Disorders of the respiratory system, such as colds, influenza and bronchitis, lung infections and sore throats were treated with it. A decongestant and an expectorant, it helped relieve asthma, chest infections and coughs.

It was found to be useful in disorders of the gut and in getting rid of worms. Garlic was also used as an aid to digestion and as a general cleanser of the digestive system.

Garlic had a beneficial effect on the liver and was useful in disorders relating to the blood. Blood pressure was reduced by it, as were blood sugar levels. Excessive blood clotting was also relieved by it.

Used externally when crushed, macerated in oil or made into an ointment, it was found effective in the relief of cuts, stings and bites, and ringworm. Inflamed joints and rheumatism also benefited from it, as did sprains. It was rubbed on the chest to ease chest infections and was used in the cure of earache.

ginger

Ginger root was used in Chinese medicine for about two thousand years. It was brought to England about 1600.

It was thought to have many powers, including the ability to cure frigidity in women and to act as an aphrodisiac generally.

High blood pressure was thought to be relieved by it and, although it was later taken internally to effect a cure, ginger was originally reduced to a paste with water and applied to the forehead to bring down blood pressure.

Ginger was used to stimulate the heart and circulation. It was used in respiratory disorders, such as colds or flu, as an expectorant, and to bring down a fever.

It was particularly noted for its use in the treatment of disorders of the digestive system, being used to prevent or cure nausea, relieve flatulence and diarrhoea, and aid digestion.

Menstrual problems were also treated with it. It was used to promote the menstrual flow in cases of delayed periods.

Ginger was thought to be an aid to fertility. Impotence was also treated with it.

It was found to be useful in disorders of the blood, being used to prevent excessive blood clotting and to reduce blood pressure.

The ageing process was thought to be slowed down by the taking of ginger.

Externally ginger was used in liniments to ease the pain of lumbago, and painful joints generally, and neuralgia. Chewing a piece of fresh ginger was thought to relieve toothache.

gipsywort

The dried flowers of gipsywort were used in an infusion to prevent blood clotting, to reduce the pulse rate and as a sedative in cases of heart disease and high blood pressure.

glycerine

Glycerine is a colourless sticky liquid that was obtained by heating and distilling fats.

It was once used in the treatment of tuberculosis or consumption, also being used to relieve dry coughs. Disorders of the digestive system and bowel were also treated by it. Colic was thought to be relieved by it, as were indigestion and flatulence. It was effective as a laxative and as a bowel relaxant.

Externally it was used to moisturize and soothe the skin and was used to relieve inflammation in eczema, burns and chilblains. Used with rose water, it was applied for the relief of chapped lips or sunburn. Used with lavender oil it was good for healing cuts and sores.

golden rod

Golden rod is also known as Aaron's rod or woundwort.

Early herbalists used it to heal wounds, the reason for one of the names given to the plant.

Later it was used as a diuretic and to dissolve kidney stones and gall stones. It was also used to stop vomiting and to aid digestion. Diphtheria was also thought to be helped by it.

gout

Golden rod was used to help painful menstruation and to encourage the menstrual flow in cases of amenorrhoea. Catarrh was also treated with it, and it was used to induce perspiration and as an antiseptic.

golden rod

gout

A clove of garlic eaten night and morning was thought to be a cure for gout. Watercress, carrot, apple, leeks,

cucumber, onion and turnip were all used in its treatment.

Parsley, dandelion, burdock, nettle, dock, marigold, rosemary, sage, thyme, hawthorn and borage were used as a cure for the symptoms of gout. Elder and meadowsweet were also used.

A bath with Epsom salts was thought to relieve the symptoms of gout. Raw potato juice and hot potato water were once applied to painful areas in gout. The bruised fresh leaves of peppermint or a lotion made from these were used to apply to sore areas in gout.

ground elder

An infusion of the fresh leaves of ground elder was used as a diuretic, as a sedative and as a pain reliever. It was thought to relieve gout, sciatica and rheumatism.

groundsel

Groundsel was used by early herbalists to treat painful menstruation. It was later used as a laxative or purgative and was thought to cure stomach ache. The plant was used as an emetic.

Biliousness was treated with it. It was also used in cases where the body temperature had to be lowered.

Externally, groundsel was used in hot poultices on boils and in cold poultices for nursing mothers to relieve engorged breasts. It was also used externally for cleaning wounds and healing chapped hands as well as for treating bleeding gums.

groundsel

ground ivy
The dried flowers of ground ivy were used in an infusion as an expectorant in catarrh and bronchitis and as a diuretic. Ground ivy was also used to cure cystitis and sciatica and as a gargle for sore throats.

gums, bleeding
Witch hazel was used as a mouthwash for bleeding gums, as were borage, rosemary and meadowsweet. A decoction of the root of comfrey or an infusion of the leaves of comfrey was also used in this way.

Another mouthwash for bleeding gums consisted of cold tea. An infusion of olive leaves was also used.

H

haemorrhoids

A common name for haemorrhoids is piles.

An infusion of watercress applied externally as a lotion was considered to be helpful in cases of piles. An external application of crushed fresh leaves of plantain was also used, as was a poultice or compress of witch hazel. Yarrow and marigold applied externally were used as treatments also, and meadowsweet was one of the earliest cures for the condition.

Eating carrots was used as a treatment for piles, as was eating oats. Another cure recommended eating a large leek, and another involved taking a glass of a liquid made from nettles several times a day.

hair

There were several traditional treatments for improving the condition of the hair. Washing the hair with egg was one of these, and castor oil was another well-known hair conditioner.

Applying an infusion of fresh nettle leaves was meant to have a beneficial effect on the hair. Fresh parsley juice was thought to make the hair shiny, and a decoction of burdock was massaged into the scalp as a hair tonic.

An infusion of chamomile flowers was meant to be an effective hair tonic, the scalp being cleansed with it twice a week. Another infusion made with sage, rosemary, honeysuckle and plantain with added honey was used as a hair wash to improve the condition of the hair. A strong infusion of sage alone was recommended as a hair tonic, and this was also meant to cure dandruff.

Hair fall was frequently treated with folk remedies. Again, egg was recommended. Fresh eggs were to be beaten, rubbed into the hair and left overnight. Damping the hair with an infusion of sage was also said to help prevent hair falling out.

Dilute rosemary oil rubbed on the scalp was also meant to stop hair falling out, and castor oil applied in the same way was also meant to be effective. A rinse made from yarrow was also used to prevent hair fall, and a mixture of boxwood, rosemary and marshmallow added to boiling water had the same claims made for it.

A mixture of kerosene and water used in equal parts was used in the cure of dandruff but it was also claimed to be able to stop the hair from growing grey if it was applied before the hair started to grow grey.

See also BALDNESS; DANDRUFF.

halitosis

Avens, dill and peppermint were used as a cure for halitosis or bad breath.

Halitosis may be caused by some disorder of the stomach. To avoid this, one suggested remedy involved taking a powder containing powdered vegetable charcoal and bicarbonate of soda.

hands, chapped

One remedy considered to be effective for chapped hands involved taking a piece of mutton fat, melting it and straining it and pouring it into a basin to harden it. Before it was quite hardened, it was worked into a ball. This ball was then held before a fire until the surface of the ball began to soften. The substance was then worked into the hands.

Another folk cure was a bit more complicated. Some unsalted hog's lard was washed in spring water and then rose water. It was then mixed with egg yolks and honey before fine oatmeal was mixed into it to form a paste. This was rubbed into the hands.

hangover

Eating raw cabbage was an old folk cure for hangovers. Rosemary is also an old remedy.

Drinking a lot of water was also thought to be an effective cure, and some people recommended eating raw beaten egg.

hawthorn

hawthorn

Common names for hawthorn are may and whitethorn.

In early times hawthorn was supposed to have the power to ward off witches and evil spirits. Young girls bathed in the dew that formed on it on the morning of the first day of May in the hope of improving their complexions.

Some people claimed that the smell of hawthorn had aphrodisiac properties.

Hawthorn was used as a heart stimulant and tonic. It was recommended in cases of low blood pressure and was used as a diuretic in cases of dropsy and kidney disorders.

A decoction of the flowers and berries was used as a cure for sore throats. It was also used for chilblains.

hay fever

Clove tea was thought to relieve the symptoms of hay fever. An infusion of plantain was also given for the relief of these, as was an infusion of nettles. A hot infusion of balm was also taken to bring relief to the hay fever sufferer.

Adding chamomile to boiling water and inhaling the steam from this was also recommended to alleviate the symptoms of hay fever.

One folk cure for hay fever involved soaking some elecampane, also called elfwort, in boiling water, straining it and taking a glass of it at regular intervals until the symptoms disappeared.

headache

An old English superstition recommended not a cure
for headaches but a supposed method of avoiding them.
No hair that had either been cut from the head or that
had fallen out of its own accord was to be thrown away
in a careless manner. If the hair was carelessly discarded,
the fear was that a bird would find the hair and carry it
off and use it for nest-building. Apparently, if this hap-
pened the head of the owner of the hair would ache all
the time that the bird was building the nest.

Whether the headache was acquired in this way or in
a more mundane way, there were several folk remedies
for headaches.

An infusion made from elderflowers was held to be a
cure for a headache, as was an infusion of lime flowers, an
infusion of dried rosemary or an infusion of chamomile.
A tea made from betony was also regarded as curative.

A more complicated cure involved taking some centaury, feverfew and chamomile and boiling them in water until the liquid was reduced by half. Some rhubarb
was added to the hot liquid.

Another cure had coltsfoot as a base. The coltsfoot
leaves were boiled in water and sweetened with a syrup
made from sugar and water. A cupful of this was to be
drunk. This was a versatile cure as it was a remedy for
coughs, colds and giddiness as well as headaches.

The Greeks and Romans used peppermint as a cure

for headaches. Later, cures taken internally included cinnamon, honey, and apple. Rosemary, chamomile, dock, lavender, balm and meadowsweet were herbs that were taken internally as a cure.

Other herbs that were used in the cure of headaches were angelica, basil, betony, feverfew, pennyroyal, St John's wort, valerian, viper's bugloss and wintergreen.

Externally applied, fresh elder leaves were thought to be curative, as were slices of raw potato, cabbage poultices and onion poultices. Clove oil could be rubbed on the temples, as could lavender oil and vinegar. Clove oil could also be used as an inhalant.

A preventative for headaches dating from the fifteenth century involved distilling a mixture of vervain, betony and wormwood and then washing the head in it several times a week.

A solution for washing the head to cure headaches consisted of mixing salt, vinegar, water and brandy. A towel soaked in very hot water, wrung out and wound round the head was meant to bring quite quick relief.

head lice

Cinnamon applied externally as a wash was thought to get rid of head lice. They were also meant to be cured by the application of fresh parsley juice. Rosemary oil was thought to be helpful in the treatment of head lice.

A non-herbal treatment to get rid of nits involved

mixing kerosene and water in equal parts and applying the lotion to the hair.

heartburn

One suggested method of avoiding heartburn was to take a teaspoonful of wheat charcoal immediately after it. It was suggested that this treatment was backed up by taking a spoonful of glycerine either before or after meals.

A suggested cure for heartburn consisted of a mixture made from ginger, quassia, sal volatile and sulphite of soda. Another, probably more popular, remedy was the taking of a spoonful of whisky in warm water with meals.

Although lemon is usually regarded as acidic, it was used in many digestive problems, heartburn included. Eggs were used as a cure for heartburn, as the white of the egg was thought to be a soothing influence. Peppermint was a popular cure.

Raw cabbage was considered to be beneficial, and rose tea was once thought to alleviate the condition. Meadowsweet, taken internally, was also used to treat heartburn.

heart problems

Hawthorn was thought to have curative powers as far as heart disease was concerned. One remedy consisted of making an infusion of dried hawthorn leaves with added honey.

Centaury was the basis of another cure. It was boiled in beer, strained and sweetened with honey. It was to be taken three times a day.

Herbs and plants that were considered to be helpful in heart disorders included asparagus, butterbur, broom, bugle, burnet, figwort and gipsywort. Others included lily of the valley, motherwort, raspberry, viper's bugloss and woodruff.

Tea, carrots, onions and olive oil taken internally were also thought to be beneficial in heart problems.

heartsease

Heartsease was long regarded as a remedy for epilepsy. It was also used as a treatment for catarrh and asthma.

Disorders of the blood and heart disease were treated with it, and it was known as a diuretic.

A decoction of the flowers was used to cure some skin complaints.

herb robert

Herb robert is also known as red robin and St Robert's herb. It was used widely in medieval folk medicine and has been used in various ways since medieval times.

Skin complaints were treated with it, and it was used in the treatment of bruises and to reduce swelling. A lotion for eye problems was made from it, and it was used as a gargle for sore throats and mouth ulcers.

It was used in the treatment of diarrhoea.

herb robert

hiccups

A very old cure for hiccups was a hot infusion of white mustard seeds. Taking lemon was also supposed to help, and cloves were meant to be beneficial. Peppermint was a very popular cure, as was simple hot water.

One cure advocated drinking three sips of cold water from the far side of a cup. Another also involving water recommended placing the fingers in the ears while drinking a lot of cold water. Alternatively, a pinch of snuff could be taken in an effort to cure hiccups.

Rather a strange cure involved taking three or four preserved damsons in the mouth at once and swallowing them gradually.

honey

Honey was thought to be highly nutritious and was particularly recommended for people who had been ill to give them energy. A remedy advocated for delicate children consisted of boiled milk with added honey.

It was also used as a sedative and to promote relaxation and sleep, and as such was sometimes used in cases of insomnia. Again, it was sometimes added to hot milk and taken just before going to bed.

Honey was considered to be a very versatile substance in folk medicine. It was, for example, thought to relieve the pain of headaches, neuralgia or arthritis.

It was frequently used as an expectorant and was helpful in the treatment of coughs and catarrh. It was sometimes used with hot lemon to soothe sore throats, and is often used in this way today. Herbs, such as thyme, were sometimes added to it to relieve the symptoms of asthma or bronchitis. Honey was thought to have the power to relieve congestion, and was used in the treatment of sinusitis, and hay fever.

honeysuckle

Diarrhoea and vomiting were treated with it, and it was thought to help in the treatment of various infections, such as typhoid.

Externally, honey was used as a treatment for burns and as a means of bringing boils to a head. It was also thought to speed up the cure of sores or ulcers in the mouth. Wounds were once spread with honey in the belief that it would aid healing.

In early times honey was regarded as an aphrodisiac.

honeysuckle

Honeysuckle is also known as goat's leaf.

It was used as an expectorant, being used in respiratory disorders and asthma. Disorders of the liver and spleen were also treated with it, and it was used as a gargle.

Constipation was treated with it, since honeysuckle was thought to have laxative properties.

hops

Hops are also known as hop bine or willow wolf.

Hops have been used since medieval times in the brewing of beer, and they are probably best known for that today. They had, however, several uses in folk medicine.

They were probably best known as a cure for insomnia, having strong sedative properties, and were also used in nervous disorders. However, they were also used in indigestion, disorders of the stomach and as a stimulant

honeysuckle

of the appetite. Heart disease, liver disorders and jaundice were also treated by them.

Externally they were used to treat bruises and reduce inflammation and swelling, often in combination with chamomile.

horehound, white
White horehound is also known as horehound or hoarhound.

It was used as a cure for coughs in ancient Egypt and

123

thereafter. It was also used in the treatment of catarrh, bronchitis, diseases of the lung, and asthma.

Constipation was treated with it. Horehound was also used to stop the menstrual flow or to decrease it.

It was used externally on cuts, bruises and in the treatment of minor skin conditions.

horseradish

We now know horseradish as an accompaniment to roast beef, but it was used in several treatments in folk medicine.

It was used to stimulate the appetite and to cure flatulence. Urinary infections and colds and influenza were also treated with it.

Externally, it was used to cure chilblains and boils.

horsetail

Horsetail was also known as sharegrass and bottlebrush.

It was used to treat kidney and bladder disorders and urinary infections. Disorders of the prostate gland and some disorders of the digestive system were also treated with it.

Externally, it was used in the curing of open sores, wounds and chilblains.

hypertension

A more common, less technical, name for hypertension is high blood pressure.

Various herbs were thought to be effective in the lowering of blood pressure. These included barberry, chervil, comfrey, garlic and hawthorn. Parsley, rue, skullcap, vervain and violet were also thought to be effective.

Cinnamon, ginger, and olive oil were used in the treatment of high blood pressure, as were apples, potatoes, onions and leeks. The condition was also treated with yarrow, balm and lavender.

hypotension

A more common, less technical, name for hypotension is low blood pressure.

Hawthorn was used in the treatment of low blood pressure to try to bring it up to normal levels. Broom, lavender, rosemary and shepherd's purse were also used.

hyssop

Hyssop was used as a cure for chronic catarrh and asthma. In the case of asthma it was sometimes taken in conjunction with horehound. It was also used in the treatment of stomach disorders.

Externally, it was used to ease bruises, cuts and pain caused by muscular rheumatism.

hysteria

One cure recommended strong tansy tea, taken cold, as a cure for hysteria. Another cure suggested mixing chamomile, valerian, lime flowers and St John's wort to make an infusion to be taken three times a day.

Herbs thought to be useful in cases of hysteria included betony, catnip, centaury, lady's bedstraw, lavender and lily of the valley. Peppermint, motherwort, poppy, skullcap, valerian, vervain, viper's bugloss and watercress were also used.

I

impotence

Cinnamon was used as a remedy for impotence in folk medicine, as was ginger. Rose petals and oats were also thought to improve the condition.

See also FERTILITY.

indigestion

Dill, fennel and feverfew were used as remedies for indigestion in folk medicine. Peppermint, speedwell and thyme were also used.

Ginger and peppermint were both popular cures for indigestion. The juice of a raw potato was also considered to be instrumental in curing indigestion as was egg white. Apple and tea were also popular, and another remedy was Epsom salts.

Cloves were also considered to be a remedy for indigestion. Olive oil and cardamom seeds were used to treat it, and parsley and burdock taken internally were thought to be beneficial. The symptoms of indigestion

inflammation

was also thought to be relieved by lavender and mead-owsweet.

See also DIGESTION, AIDS TO.

inflammation

Oatmeal used externally was used in the reduction of inflammation, as was raw potato juice. Pepper was thought to bring inflammation to the surface and to relieve pain. Vinegar was also used to reduce inflammation, as was a combination of hops and chamomile applied externally.

A poultice made from barley flour was another suggested cure. Other poultice cures were made from plantain, burdock or eucalyptus leaves.

Crushed fresh leaves of plantain and cucumber juice were both used to soothe inflamed skin, as were dock leaves. Meadowsweet flowers and elderflowers were also used.

Lavender oil and chamomile oil were both used in inflammatory skin conditions.

insomnia

Honey in milk with a pinch of nutmeg or cinnamon taken before going to bed was a well-known cure for insomnia. A teaspoon of honey on its own was also recommended or honey taken with cider vinegar.

Hops have been used as a cure for insomnia since the

Middle Ages. Chamomile was known as a relaxant and was a common cure for sleeplessness, as were lavender and lemon balm. Hawthorn was also thought conducive to sleep, and rosemary was an old folk cure for insomnia.

Poppy and valerian were also used to induce sleep, as were skullcap and woodruff. Dandelion, dill and peppermint were also used.

Eating onions at bedtime was also a recommended cure. Either stewed Spanish onions or ordinary raw onions would do, and two or three of them were to be taken. Onion soup or onion jelly was a suggested alternative. Onion jelly was made by shredding onions and cooking them in a little stock until the onions were tender. Boiling water and a squeeze of lemon were added and the mixture cooked together.

Mattresses were sometimes stuffed with oat husks as a cure for insomnia.

iodine

Iodine is an element that has been used in home remedies for more than a hundred years.

It was used in the treatment of skin infections and to stop cuts and sores becoming infected.

itching

One old cure for itching involved using a piece of cacao

butter impregnated with cocaine. This was to be rubbed over the itchy part. The butter would melt on the warm skin, making a smooth, soothing cover.

Alternative cures were a weak carbolic acid lotion or a solution of bicarbonate of soda.

See also STINGS AND BITES.

J

Jacob's ladder

Other common names for the Jacob's ladder plant are charity and Greek valerian.

It was used in the treatment of coughs, colds, chest complaints, lung complaints and pleurisy, especially as an expectorant. It induced perspiration and cured fevers.

jaundice

In early European folk medicine parsley was used as a cure for jaundice. The root of the dandelion was also thought to be effective, and hops were also used.

One cure for jaundice consisted of dandelion flowers, blue cornflowers and parsley crushed together in some beer. This was to be taken night and morning.

Another cure was an infusion of agrimony taken three times a day.

One particularly unpleasant old cure in folk medicine involved the patient eating a slice of bread and butter with nine lice on it.

juniper

juniper

The berries and leaves of juniper were used in herbal medicine, although now the herb is most commonly known in the kitchen, since the berries are used to flavour certain dishes.

Juniper was used to treat indigestion and flatulence. It was also used in the curing of kidney and bladder conditions and, being a diuretic, was particularly effective in curing dropsy. It was sometimes used in conjunction with other diuretics.

K

kidney problems

Pepper was used in the treatment of kidney disorders, as was rose-hip syrup. Meadowsweet was also used.

Other herbs used in the treatment of kidney disorders included agrimony, angelica, bearberry, betony, broom, daisy, dandelion and fumitory. Golden rod, hawthorn, horsetail, hyssop, juniper, kidneywort, parsley, shepherd's purse and strawberry were also thought to be beneficial.

A drink made from lime water and pearl barley water was thought to be helpful in kidney disease. Another remedial drink consisted of boiling nettle leaves in water, straining it and fermenting the liquid to make a nettle beer. Cloves, ginger, honey and brown sugar were added to this.

An infusion made from several herbs was thought to relieve disorders of the kidney. The herbs were burdock seeds, dandelion, marshmallow root and tansy.

See also DIURETICS; URINARY PROBLEMS.

kidneywort

Other common names for this plant are pennywort and liverwort.

Medieval herbalists used it to treat disorders of the kidneys, hence its name. In early folk medicine it was used to treat gout.

Kidneywort is a diuretic and is also used to reduce inflammation. It was particularly used to reduce inflammation in the liver and spleen and was thought to be beneficial in cases of gout and sciatica. Bronchitis was sometimes treated by it.

The bruised leaves were applied in a poultice to cure piles and to treat minor burns or scalds and pimples and sores. Kidneywort was also used in some eye treatments.

knotgrass

Knotgrass is also known as pigweed, cowgrass, all-seed, birdweed and bird's tongue.

It was used to cure internal bleeding and to reduce excessive menstrual flow. The fresh juice was squirted up the nostrils to stop nose bleeding.

Diarrhoea and dysentery were also thought to be cured by it. It was used as a remedy for bronchitis and lung diseases and in the treatment of jaundice. Piles were treated with it, and it was thought to have the power to dissolve kidney stones and gall stones.

L

lady's bedstraw

Lady's bedstraw is also known as wild rosemary and maiden's hair.

It was used in folk medicine as a sedative. Hysteria and nervous conditions were treated by it, as was epilepsy.

Lady's bedstraw was also used as a tonic and as a diuretic. It was once used as an insect repellent.

larch

The inner bark of the larch was used medicinally in traditional herbal medicine. It had various uses.

It was used as a diuretic and in the treatment of cystitis. Bronchitis was treated with it, and it was a noted expectorant. Larch was used to treat internal bleeding and as an antidote to some poisons.

Externally it was used in the treatment of eczema and psoriasis.

lady's bedstraw

lavender

Lavender is known as English lavender and garden lavender.

Its name is derived from the Latin for 'to wash', and it got its name from the fact that the Romans used it in their baths. They also placed it in linen bags among their clothes to perfume them and take away any unpleasant odours.

In the Middle Ages lavender oil was used to kill lice and bed bugs. It was also used to clean wounds.

Lavender was used as an antiseptic in such disorders as diphtheria. It was also a mild diuretic and was used in disorders in which there was fluid retention. Colds, catarrh, and chest infections were treated by it since it was a decongestant and expectorant. It was also used to induce perspiration and bring down fevers.

It was well known as a sedative in cases of excessive nervousness, anxiety and heart palpitations, and insomnia and headaches were thought to be relieved by it. On the other hand, it was also used as a stimulant to the nervous system, and it was used to lift the spirits of people who were feeling depressed and to stimulate the appetite. Low blood pressure and dizziness were thought to be helped by lavender.

Disorders of the digestive system were treated with lavender. It was thought to be helpful in curing flatulence, colic, indigestion and nausea. Lavender was thought to relieve pain, and it was used for the relief of toothache as well as for headaches.

It had several external uses, especially in the form of an oil. One of these was as an insect repellent. Another one was as a soother of inflammation, and it was also used to relieve bruises and sprains and to soothe swollen joints. Lavender was also used to cure cuts, sores and wounds.

laxative

Apple, olive oil, rose-hip syrup and oats were used for their laxative properties. Elderberries, plantain seeds and flax were also used as laxatives. White mustard seeds were also once used.

Dock was used as a laxative for the treatment of long-term constipation, and dandelion root was used where a mild laxative was called for. Epsom salts was used when a fast-working laxative was required.

Asparagus, buckthorn, chickweed, fat hen, feverfew, groundsel and liquorice were some of the herbs that were thought to act as laxatives.

leeks

Eating leeks was one of the folk remedies for haemorrhoids.

Anyone who had swallowed anything sharp was encouraged to eat boiled leeks to prevent the sharp object from damaging the stomach or bowel before it was expelled from the body.

Leeks were also used as a cough remedy, being expectorants and decongestants. They were used in the relief of colds, catarrh, chest infections, hoarseness and sore throats.

The leek was also a diuretic and was used in the treatment of gout, arthritis and cystitis. It was also used in treatment of disorders of the digestive system, such as colic and diarrhoea. Some forms of heart disease were also treated by it.

A poultice made from leeks was used as a dressing

for wounds and sores. A paste of mashed cooked leaves was used to bring boils to a head. An application of leeks was used to spread on burns and inflamed skin to soothe the skin. A cut leek rubbed on an insect sting was meant to relieve the pain of the sting.

lemon

Lemon was used in various ways in folk medicine, and it has been credited with curative powers for a very long time. The Romans used it as an antidote to all poisons.

Although it is usually thought of as being acidic, it was used in hot water as a cure for biliousness. Lemon was also used for disorders of the digestive system, including hiccups, heartburn and nausea, and for disorders of the bowel, such as constipation and worms.

Lemon juice taken in the morning acted as a stimulant of bile and so as a tonic to the liver. It was also used to dissolve gall stones. It was thought to be a remedy for various infections and as a means of bringing down fever. Asthma was thought to be relieved by it, as were sore throats and tonsillitis.

Lemon was also used as a diuretic and as a cure for arthritis and rheumatism. Mixed with coffee it was thought to be effective in the treatment of malaria. This mixture was also used as a treatment for headaches.

Externally lemon was used as an astringent to stem bleeding. If some lemon juice was put on a piece of cotton wool and then applied to the nostrils it would stop nose bleeds. It was also used to massage bleeding gums.

Lemon juice was also used to prevent sunburn. When mixed with glycerine it was used to soothe chapped lips.

lemon balm *see* balm.

lettuce, wild
Wild lettuce is also called green endive.

It was used in herbal medicine as a sedative and to induce sleep. Colic was treated with it, as were irritable coughs. It was a diuretic and was used in dropsy.

lice, head *see* head.

lilac
Lilac was used medicinally as a diuretic and to reduce inflammation. It was principally used in the treatment of fevers, especially malaria, and was also used to relieve rheumatism.

lily of the valley
Lily of the valley is also known as May blossom and wood lily.

Its main use was as a heart stimulant, like the foxglove, but it was also used to treat sinusitis and dizziness in cases of fluid retention. Externally it was used for rheumatic pain.

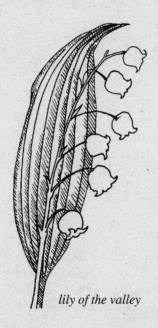

lily of the valley

lime tree
Early herbalists used a tea distilled from the flowers of lime as a cure for epilepsy. It was even thought that just sitting under a lime tree could cure people of epileptic fits.

141

linseed

It was used in the treatment of low blood pressure and to cure certain nervous disorders. Catarrh, coughs and headaches were all thought to be eased by it, as were fevers.

Externally it was used on the skin to soothe rashes.

linseed see flax.

lips, chapped

A mixture of glycerine and lemon juice was recommended for chapped lips. Alternative cures included an oil made from rose, an ointment made from rose, or a mixture of glycerine and rose water.

liquorice

The ancient Greeks used liquorice to quench their thirst. Being much sweeter than sugar, it was used by early herbalists to sweeten some of their potions that contained bitter herbs. It was also used as a cough medicine, being an expectorant, and later as a cure for sore throats, chest complaints and consumption, or tuberculosis, and asthma.

It was also used to treat indigestion and ulcers.

liver problems

The juice of raw potato taken internally was used in disorders of the liver, as was raw onion. Apple was also thought to be helpful. Herbs believed to be beneficial in disorders of the liver included agrimony, avens, daisy, sage and rosemary.

lockjaw

One old cure for lockjaw involved pouring a little warm turpentine into the wound that had caused, or might cause, lockjaw. Another cure for lockjaw involved smoking the wound in the smoke from burning wool.

To prevent lockjaw, it was suggested that the wound should be made to bleed copiously until it became numb. Suggestions to make it bleed included tapping the wound with a stick or knife handle.

lovage

Lovage is also known as sea parsley.

Being rich in vitamin C, it was used as a cure for scurvy. It was also used as a diuretic and a stimulant.

lung problems

Herbs that were used to cure or relieve lung disease included comfrey, knotgrass and primrose, while an old cure for tuberculosis was made up of honey and horseradish.

M

madder

In folk medicine this plant was much used in the treatment of kidney stones. It was also used to cure gall stones and as a remedy for fluid retention and urinary disorders. Madder was also thought to have laxative properties.

Externally it was applied to wounds to clean them.

malaria

One old cure for malaria was lemon taken in coffee. The early herbalists treated malaria with the roots of parsley, and eucalyptus was the basis of another old remedy.

Malaria was often in the past known as ague. Other remedies are given in the entry on ague.

See also AGUE.

marigold

Taken internally, marigold was used in the treatment of low blood pressure, as an aperient and as a mild sedative. It was also thought to have the power to stop pus from forming and was used to treat ulcers and varicose veins.

As an external application it was used from early times to relieve the pain and reduce the swelling of insect stings, particularly those of wasps. It was used in skin rashes and other skin disorders to reduce inflammation and on burns to soothe them.

An application of marigold was used to relieve eyes that were sore and inflamed. It was used particularly in cases of conjunctivitis.

It was used externally as a treatment for warts.

marjoram

The ancient Greeks are said to have planted marjoram over the tombs of the dead to bring peace to their spirits and prevent them from coming back to haunt the living. In early folk belief marjoram may have been thought to have the power to increase fertility, as newly married couples had coronets made from marjoram flowers placed on their heads. Nowadays it is best known as a culinary herb but it had several uses in herbal medicine.

It was thought to have the power to cleanse the body of impurities, to purify the blood and to induce perspiration. Measles were treated with it as it was thought to bring out the spots.

Colic was thought to be relieved by it, as were sea-sickness and stomach upsets. It was used as a sedative, as a remedy for some nervous conditions, and as a stimulant of the appetite. Bronchitis and deafness were thought to respond to treatment by it.

Toothache was considered to be relieved by it if marjoram was applied to the aching tooth externally. Marjoram was also used externally as a liniment and in poultices to bring down swelling and relieve rheumatism.

marshmallow

Marshmallow has been used in folk medicine for a long time, being used by the ancient Greeks. In the Middle Ages it was used as a remedy for venereal disease, but many other cures were also associated with it.

When it is put in water, the root of the marshmallow swells to form a gel that was used to soothe burns and cuts, rashes and skin diseases. It was also used to reduce inflammation.

Applied in a poultice it was used to treat troublesome insect bites. A lotion made from the root or leaves was used in the treatment of dandruff.

The dried root boiled in milk was used as a remedy for whooping cough and bronchitis. Marshmallow taken internally was also used in urinary disorders.

meadowsweet

Meadowsweet was originally used as a flavouring for mead. In early folklore it was thought to induce such a deep sleep that it could lead to death.

It was used in the treatment of stomach disorders and as a remedy for ulcers, colic and heartburn. The herb was thought to be effective as a remedy for diarrhoea and for dropsy, and it was used to cure disorders of the blood.

It was used as a painkiller in conditions like arthritis and rheumatism. Fevers and chills were also treated with it.

measles

Watercress taken internally was used in the treatment of measles, and a hot decoction of burdock was administered to the patient to induce perspiration and reduce the fever.

A hot infusion of marigold was used to induce perspiration and bring out the eruption in measles to speed recovery. Yarrow taken internally was also thought to bring out the spots and speed recovery, as were marjoram and myrrh. A hot infusion of elderflowers was also used to achieve the same effect.

memory, poor

Hawthorn was thought to improve the fading of the

memory caused by the ageing process or poor blood supply to the brain because of its supposed power to improve poor circulation.

Rosemary was thought to improve the blood supply to the head and was thus supposed to improve the memory as well as stimulating the brain.

Another remedy suggested that people who found difficulty in remembering things should drink a tea made from sage, sweetened to taste.

menopause
Nettle was used to relieve the symptoms of the menopause. Sage and marigold were also thought to be of benefit in the relief of menopausal symptoms and were considered to be particularly effective in treating hot flushes.

Balm was considered to be of help in relieving the depression that can accompany the menopause. Hawthorn was suggested as a remedy for the night sweats that are a common symptom of the menopause.

menstruation
Heavy bleeding in menstruation was treated with cinnamon, plantain, sage or nettles. An older remedy suggested that three or four lemons should be taken daily to reduce excessive bleeding in menstruation.

Dock and borage were used as a remedy for menstrual irregularity, and chamomile was used for this in Greek and Roman times. Other remedies were witch hazel, rose and rosemary.

Marigold and sage were used to regulate menstruation, as were carrots. Ginger, myrrh and watercress were considered to be effective in promoting menstruation and in bringing on delayed periods.

Painful periods were thought to be relieved by a number of herbs. These included groundsel, lavender, mother-wort, pennyroyal, rue and skullcap.

milk

Milk was commonly used to ease indigestion and to relieve the pain caused by stomach ulcers.

It was also thought to have a soothing effect on the skin and was used as a face wash in an effort to improve the complexion.

mistletoe

Mistletoe is now associated with Christmas and kissing under the mistletoe, but it was used quite extensively in folk medicine.

It was used as a remedy for epilepsy and for other conditions that were characterized by convulsions. Low blood pressure was thought to be helped by it, and it was used in the treatment of some malignant tumours.

Nervous disorders and hysteria were treated with mistletoe, and it was used in cases of delirium. Mistletoe

motherwort

was considered a remedy for urinary complaints and chronic arthritis.

mistletoe

motherwort

Another name for motherwort is lion's tail.

It was used by the Greeks as a nerve tonic for pregnant women. The herb was also used by early herbalists to treat menstrual irregularity and problems that occurred in childbirth, and as a cure for vaginal infections.

In early folklore motherwort was considered to be an aid to a long life if eaten regularly.

Motherwort was used to treat heart conditions and as a remedy for epilepsy. Low blood pressure was thought to benefit from its use. It was used as a sedative and thought to be a remedy for hysteria and excessive nervousness.

mullein

Mullein was used by early herbalists as a cure for gout and piles. Because of its rather unpleasant bitter taste it was often mixed with another herb to improve the taste.

It was commonly used in disorders of the respiratory system, being used to treat asthma and bronchitis.

The herb had several external applications. A poultice made from the leaves or flowers was used to relieve burns. A mixture of mullein leaves, hot vinegar and water was used to treat haemorrhoids. The leaves were also boiled with lard or vegetable fat to make an ointment to be applied to wounds to speed the healing process.

mustard

White mustard seeds were used in early times as a treatment for disorders of the digestive system and as a laxative for chronic constipation. An infusion of white mustard seeds and hot water was also used as a cure for whooping cough.

Mustard was also used to improve poor circulation, to relieve colds, influenza and chest infections, to cure chilblains, and to raise the spirits of people who had depression. It was used to induce vomiting in cases of poisoning.

A hot mustard foot bath was thought to relieve congestion in head or chest colds, and an infusion of mustard was used as a gargle for sore throats.

myrrh

Myrrh was burned as an old remedy for getting rid of fleas.

Later it was used as a tonic for people who required to have their strength built up. It was thought to improve circulation and to be an effective decongestant and expectorant in respiratory disease, such as bronchitis, catarrh, colds and tuberculosis. In diseases that involved a rash, myrrh was thought to push the eruption to the surface and speed recovery.

The appetite was thought to be stimulated by it, and it was meant to improve digestion and cure flatulence. It was thought to be effective against intestinal parasites.

Myrrh was used to regulate late periods and was used as a relaxant to relieve spasm. It was also used to induce contractions when childbirth was thought to be imminent, and therefore was not used by pregnant women unless the birth was due.

Externally it was used as a gargle and a mouthwash and to bring relief for minor injuries.

N

nausea

Ginger and peppermint have long been held to be excellent cures for nausea. Cinnamon, cloves, chamomile, sage and cardamom were all thought to be effective remedies for it also. Lemon, rose-hip syrup and lavender were also used as remedies for nausea.

Rosemary leaves mixed with an equal amount of honey was recommended. A cup of hot water taken before meals was thought to prevent nausea.

nervous problems

Raw cabbage was an old cure for nervous disorders, and lavender was noted for its calming effect. Cinnamon was used as a remedy for nervous problems while yarrow was used to reduce anxiety. Honey was thought to have a calming effect.

See also HYSTERIA.

nettle

Nettles were considered to be an excellent remedy for

purifying the blood. They were also once regarded as an aphrodisiac. In ancient Greece they were used as an antidote to poisoning by hemlock and as a remedy for scorpion stings and snake bites.

The nettle was used as a diuretic and was thought to lower blood pressure. Gout and arthritis were treated with nettles.

It was thought to be an aid to digestion and was used to treat some digestive disorder such as flatulence, ulcers and diarrhoea as well as to eradicate worms.

Nettles were used to reduce heavy menstrual bleeding and as a tonic during the menopause. They were taken by nursing mothers to improve their milk supply.

Respiratory problems, such as catarrh, asthma, pleurisy and lung disease, were treated with nettles. They were also used to bring down fevers.

Applied externally they were used to cure arthritis. Cuts and wounds were treated with them, as were burns and insect stings. Nettles were used as a remedy for bleeding noses and to make a gargle for sore throats. A tonic for the hair was made from them.

neuralgia

Honey, chamomile and elderberries taken internally were thought to bring relief to sufferers from neuralgia.

Applied externally to the site of the pain, ginger oil,

dilute eucalyptus oil or garlic added to olive oil were used to combat the pain of neuralgia. A compress made from sage, a poultice made from cabbage, or a hot mustard plaster were alternative remedies.

A mixture of rose water and white vinegar was used to make a lotion that was applied to the affected part. A liniment for neuralgia could be made from a mixture of methylated spirits, cedar bark, sassafras, origanum and powdered carbonate of ammonia. Brown paper was dipped in this mixture and applied to the area affected by neuralgia for a short time. If left on too long, it could cause blistering.

nose, bleeding

There were several suggested cures for nose bleeds in folk medicine.

One of these involved placing a nettle leaf on the tongue or against the roof of the mouth. Witch hazel dried and used as a snuff was another old cure, and powdered tea was once used in this way also.

A small piece of cloth soaked in vinegar and put up the nostrils was said to cure a bleeding nose, as was a cloth soaked in lemon juice. A cold lotion applied to the head while heat was applied to the feet constituted another old remedy.

A common remedy was the putting of a cold key down the back of the person suffering from the nose bleed.

More drastic was the pouring of cold water down the back. Grasping the nose with the finger and thumb to exclude air from the nose was also used as a remedy.

Cinnamon taken in a hot drink was thought to stop bleeding from the nose.

numbness
An old remedy for numbness was to wash the affected part in a decoction of mustard seed and wormwood.

O

olive oil

Olive oil had a variety of uses in folk medicine. It was used in the treatment of digestive problems such as flatulence, heartburn, indigestion, ulcers and constipation.

Respiratory problems, such as catarrh and dry coughs, were also treated by it.

Externally it was used to soothe the skin and to relieve the effects of eczema, cold sores and chapped skin. Often with the addition of garlic, it was used as a liniment for sprains or rheumatism. Warm olive oil, sometimes with the addition of a herb such as garlic, was dropped in the ear as a remedy for earache.

An infusion of the leaves of the olive tree was used for cleaning wounds or cuts and was also used as a mouthwash to cure bleeding gums.

onion

Onions were used medicinally from earliest times. They

were thought to have antiseptic properties and were used to ward off infection.

They were used to improve the circulation and purify the blood. They were thought to lower high blood pressure and were used as a remedy for blood clots. Cases of anaemia were treated with it.

They were used as an expectorant in colds, catarrh and bronchitis, and also to bring down fever in such conditions. Sinusitis and sore throats were also treated by it.

Onions were taken to aid digestion and as a tonic. They were used as a remedy for constipation and flatulence. Disorders of the liver were treated with onions. They were thought to have diuretic properties and were used as a remedy for gout and arthritis.

Externally they had several uses. Onion juice was used to treat burns, stings, animal bites, cuts, boils and abscesses. It was also used as a remedy for warts, toothache and earache. Onions were used in a poultice to cure chilblains and were thought to be a remedy for headaches when inhaled.

Onions were once considered to be an aphrodisiac.

P

palpitations

Lavender taken internally was thought to relieve the symptoms of nervousness and anxiety, one of which was palpitations. Hawthorn was used as a remedy for various heart conditions and in the treatment of palpitations.

An infusion of borage was also recommended for the condition. Peppermint was generally thought of as a heart tonic and was used in the treatment of palpitations.

pansy *see* heartsease.

paralysis

Nettle was used to stimulate the circulation and was also thought to have some effect in the treatment of paralysis. Early herbalists recommended rosemary as a remedy for paralysis.

Cowslips were used to try to help the condition, as were primroses.

According to folklore, a silver coin made from money

contributed by a certain number of people acted as a charm against paralysis.

parsley

We now know parsley as common culinary herb. However, it was also used in herbal medicine and also features in folklore. In ancient Greece and Rome sprigs of parsley were placed on tombs to bring good luck to the deceased. The Romans wore sprigs of it about their person to provide general protection, and the gladiators in ancient Rome ate parsley in an effort to boost their strength.

The Romans believed that a pregnant woman would miscarry if she ate parsley. Later it was used by women who were pregnant but who did not want to be. They used it to try to bring about abortions. It was found to have a stimulating effect on the muscles of the uterus, and pregnant women were advised to avoid it.

It was used to treat women after childbirth with a view to getting the uterus back to normal. The herb was also used to increase the milk supply in nursing mothers.

Parsley had several uses in herbal medicine. The bruised leaves were used against the plague and against diseases characterized by intermittent fevers.

It was used to treat bronchitis and asthma and to cleanse the kidneys. As a diuretic, it was used as remedy for dropsy and was advocated as a treatment for jaundice. Gout and arthritis were both treated by it.

The herb was used as a remedy for headaches and also for some nervous disorders, such as excessive anxiety. Listlessness and lack of energy were treated with it.

The herb was used to improve circulation and in the treatment of high blood pressure. Anaemia was also treated with it. It was thought to have the power to stimulate the appetite and was used as an aid to digestion.

It was regarded as being an antispasmodic and was used in the treatment of stomach cramps, colic and flatulence, as well as indigestion.

Externally, parsley was used in the treatment of stings and bites, and of cuts and wounds. Crushed fresh parsley leaves were put on the breasts of nursing mothers to relieve engorgement of the breasts.

It was used on the hair as a tonic to make the hair shine, and it was also used as a treatment for head lice. Applied locally, it was used as remedy for toothache.

pennyroyal

Pennyroyal was also called pudding grass or tickweed.

In early times pennyroyal was burnt to kill fleas.

The herb was toxic if taken in large doses, although small doses were used in the treatment of headache, indigestion and nervous disorders. It was a remedy that had to be used with great caution.

pepper

It acted as a stimulant to the uterus and so was used to bring on the menstrual flow in cases where it had been suppressed.

pennyroyal

pepper

Black pepper is made from dried unripe peppercorns. White pepper is made from ripe peppercorns that have been soaked and had their outer skins removed.

Pepper was used in early folk medicine as a remedy for the bubonic plague. It was also used in the treatment of feverish infections, such as typhus, cholera, smallpox, scarlet fever and dysentery.

From Greek and Roman times it has been used to treat colds and catarrh. They also used it to improve the digestive system.

One of the properties that pepper was regarded as having was the ability to bring down fevers by inducing perspiration. It was also regarded as being a diuretic.

Pepper was thought to improve digestion and act as a stimulant of the appetite. It was also used as a painkiller.

Externally pepper was used as a counterirritant, known as a rubefacient, to relieve the pain of painful joints in conditions such as rheumatism by bringing the inflammation to the surface. Pepper was also used as a treatment for cuts and wounds and acted as a gargle for sore throats.

peppermint

The ancient Greeks regarded peppermint as an aphrodisiac. It was an early cure for headaches, coughs and infections of the urinary tract.

Peppermint was much used in the treatment of disorders associated with the digestive system. It was used for the relief of indigestion and as a remedy for colic, heartburn and flatulence. It was thought to be effective in stimulating the appetite and was used to cure nausea and prevent vomiting. Diarrhoea was also treated with it.

An antispasmodic, peppermint was used to relax muscles and was thought to be particularly helpful in the treatment of abdominal cramps. Cholera and dysentery were treated with it.

Being thought to have the power to increase the production of perspiration, it was used in the treatment of feverish illnesses. It was recommended to be taken at the start of colds and influenza.

It was thought to have a good effect on the circulation and was used to stimulate the heart and to cure palpitations. The liver was also thought to be stimulated by the use of peppermint.

Hiccups were thought to be relieved by it. It was used to sweeten the breath, as it still is. Peppermint oil was used as an inhalant to cure dizziness and faintness.

Externally, peppermint oil was a recommended treatment for cuts and abrasions. Both the oil and the crushed fresh leaves were used to reduce joints made painful by arthritis, rheumatism and gout.

Peppermint oil was used as a gargle for sore throats, and it was applied to aching teeth to relieve the pain. It was also used in drops to relieve earache.

peptic ulcers *see* **ulcers, internal**.

periods, painful *see* **menstrual irregularities**.

perspiration

Several plants were used to induce perspiration, especially to bring down fevers in various infections.

The plants included pepper, cinnamon, ginger and lemon. Alcohol was also used to promote perspiration, as were cloves, garlic, onion, parsley, plantain, nettle and burdock. Hot rosemary tea was also thought to increase perspiration, as were rose tea, marigold tea and lavender tea.

A hot infusion of yarrow was also used, as was a hot infusion of balm. A decoction of hawthorn bark was thought to increase perspiration. An infusion of the leaves and flowers of meadowsweet was thought to do likewise. Peppermint and eucalyptus were also used.

See also BODY ODOUR.

phlegm *see* expectorants.

piles *see* haemorrhoids.

pimpernel

Pimpernel is also known as scarlet pimpernel.

In early folklore people thought that they could tell what time of day it was by looking at the pimpernel. The flowers of the plant opened early in the morning and closed in the afternoon. This system did not really work if it was raining because the flowers closed then also.

pink

The plant was sometimes called 'laughter bringer' since it was thought that it had the power to cure depression. It was also regarded as a diuretic.

It had to be used with great caution as it could be toxic.

pink

The pink is also known as clove pink or gilliflower.

It was used as a tonic and as a diuretic. Fevers were treated with it as it was thought to have the power to induce perspiration.

plague

The term plague usually applies to the bubonic plague. Several plants were used either as a supposed remedy for this or to prevent it.

Pepper was used in the treatment of the plague, as was parsley.

Onions were used to keep bubonic plague at bay. Sage was also thought in early times to have the power to prevent the plague. Thyme was strewn on the ground to try to ward off the plague, as was lavender.

plantain

Plantain is also known as ripple grass or waybread.

The plant has long been used as an external application in the treatment of wounds and sores. It was also used to bring relief to insect stings and bites, burns and scalds,

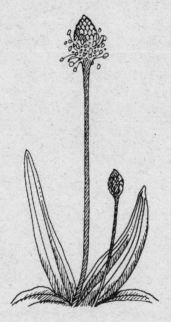

plantain

and in the treatment of sprains. The Greeks and Romans used it as a remedy against mad dog bites.

Taken internally it was regarded as having diuretic properties. It was also regarded as an expectorant and as a help for the reduction of the secretion of mucus. Because of these properties, it was considered to be a remedy for bronchitis, catarrh, colds, asthma, hay fever and sinusitis.

pleurisy

Plantain was used for relaxing spasms and as a cure for stomach and bowel infections. Diarrhoea was treated with it, and plantain seeds were used as a laxative.

It was thought to relieve heavy bleeding during menstruation and was thought to be a remedy for the vomiting of blood.

pleurisy

An old cure for pleurisy involved letting the patient bleed profusely. He or she was then advised to drink a pint of spring water to which some drops of sal ammoniac had been added.

Alcohol or vapour baths were also recommended in the treatment of pleurisy. The patient was encouraged to drink plenty of hot strong tea with catnip and to keep well covered up in bed. This was all meant to make the patient perspire freely and bring down fever.

A decoction of the roots of nettles was a traditional cure for pleurisy. Thyme taken internally was also regarded as a remedy, as was hawthorn. Pleurisy was also treated with borage, which was known for its expectorant properties and for its soothing decongestant effects.

pneumonia

Eucalyptus was used as an expectorant to bring up the phlegm in pneumonia. Thyme was often administered to relieve coughs associated with pneumonia.

Carrots were also used in old treatments for pneumonia.

See also LUNG PROBLEMS.

poison, antidotes to

As an antidote to poison an old remedy suggested stirring a heaped teaspoonful of common salt and one of ground mustard into a glass of warm water. This was swallowed quickly to induce vomiting. After the vomiting stopped, the person affected was supposed to swallow the whites of two eggs and then drink plenty of strong coffee.

Plantain was commonly used in folk medicine as a general antidote to poison, as was larch. Egg white beaten in milk was also used as an antidote, as was castor oil.

The Romans used lemons as an antidote to all poisons, and early herbalists regarded avens as an antidote.

poppy

Poppies were used as a sedative from early times, being used in the treatment of excessive nervousness, anxiety, hysteria and insomnia. It was also used for the relief of pain. Both opium and morphine are derived from the poppy. It was also used to soothe coughs and to bring down fevers by inducing perspiration. Diarrhoea and dysentery were sometimes treated with it.

potato

The juice of the raw potato was much used in traditional medicine. It was used in disorders associated with the digestive system, such as indigestion, colic, ulcers and constipation. Taken with walnut oil, potato was supposed to be an effective cure for intestinal worms. Liver disorders were also treated with it.

Potato was also used traditionally to improve the circulation. Heart disease was also thought to respond to its effects.

Raw potato juice used externally had several applications. It was used to heal wounds, ulcers and certain skin conditions. It was also used to bring relief to burns and swollen eyelids. Chilblains were treated with raw potato, as was sunburn. Slices of raw potato applied to the forehead were supposed to relieve headaches.

poultices

Poultices were a popular remedy in several conditions, especially those involving external inflammation. They were used to bring boils to a head. They were also used to bring relief to swollen joints and on the chest to relieve some respiratory or lung conditions. Inevitably they tended to be rather messy.

A poultice was a hot semi-liquid mixture spread on a piece of cloth and applied to the skin. Various substances were included in poultices, according to the purpose of the poultice and according to the properties of the substance.

A poultice that was commonly used was a bread poultice. This was made by pouring boiling water over a quantity of breadcrumbs and stirring it until the mixture formed a soft mass. This was spread about half an inch thick on a cloth and applied to the area to be covered.

Mustard formed the basis of another poultice. In this, powdered mustard was mixed to the consistency of a soft mass by the addition of cold water or vinegar. This mixture was then placed either on a piece of cloth or on a piece of brown paper.

There was a problem with mustard poultices in that they could cause blistering. For this reason it was suggested that a piece of muslin was placed between the poultice and the skin if the person being treated with the poultice had a delicate skin.

Mustard poultices were also made with one part mustard and four parts linseed meal. The mustard was mixed with warm water and the linseed meal mixed with boiling water in a separate dish. The mustard mixture was then added to the linseed meal mixture and the combined mixture applied to a piece of cloth and put on the relevant area of the patient's body.

Linseed poultices were also made without mustard. A thick paste was made by stirring the linseed meal with some boiling water. The paste was spread on a piece of cloth. It was advised that a piece of muslin dipped in olive oil could be laid on the paste to prevent it from sticking to the skin.

Yeast poultices were made by mixing a pound of ordinary flour or a pound of linseed meal with half a pint of yeast. This mixture was then heated and stirred carefully before being applied to the skin on a piece of cloth.

Charcoal poultices were made by soaking breadcrumbs in boiling water and then adding powdered wood charcoal and linseed meal. The mixture was then stirred thoroughly and applied to a piece of cloth.

Treacle poultices were less usual and were made by mixing a pound of flour with half a pint of treacle. This was then warmed, being stirred all the time, and spread on a cloth and applied in the usual way.

Several herbs and vegetables were used to make poultices. Poultices could be made from watercress and applied to wounds or boils. Raw potato slices were also made into a poultice, and this was applied to wounds and sores. Grated raw apple was used in a poultice also, often being used for ulcers.

Cabbage was also the basis of a poultice, and this was used to relieve wounds, sores and boils. Carrot poultices were also used to speed the healing process of wounds and to bring boils to a head.

Leek poultices, onion poultices, turnip poultices, burdock poultices and comfrey poultices were also used for the relief of various conditions. A poultice of the leaves and flowers of borage was a remedy for some skin conditions.

primrose

According to early folklore children who ate primroses were thought to have the power to see fairies.

Early herbalists used the primrose in the treatment of paralysis and as a remedy for gout and muscular rheumatism. It was used to reduce swelling and relieve bruises, and was also used to heal wounds and cuts.

Taken internally, primrose was used to treat nervous disorders and insomnia. Nervous headaches were treated with it, and it was used as an emetic and to expel intestinal worms.

Primrose was used to relieve lung congestion and in the treatment of bronchitis.

psoriasis

The bark and root of the elder were used in the treatment of psoriasis when applied externally to the affected area. A decoction of dock was also thought to help. Taken internally, watercress was thought to assist in the cure of psoriasis by purifying the blood.

purple loosestrife

Purple loosestrife is also called willowherb.

purple loosestrife

In early folklore purple loosestrife was said to confer psychic powers on people and to have the ability to keep away flies and insects.

It was widely used in folk medicine as an antiseptic, being used to clean wounds. Gargles for sore throats were made from it, and it was also used as a tonic.

R

rabies

The root of the elecampane was used to treat someone who had been bitten by a dog that was thought to be rabid. The elecampane root was sliced or bruised, added to a pint of milk, boiled, strained and cooled. The person being treated had to drink the liquid and fast for six hours. The treatment was to be repeated the next day and the day after that.

ragwort

Ragwort is also known as fireweed.

The leaves were used in poultices to soothe the skin and ease inflammation. Ragwort poultices were also used to bring relief to swollen joints and as a remedy for gout, sciatica and rheumatism.

The juice was used as a wash to heal burns, sores, ulcers and inflammation of the eye. A decoction of its root was used as a remedy for internal bruising. Ragwort was also used as a gargle for throat ulcers and mouth ulcers.

ragwort

raspberry

Early herbalists treated severe cases of insomnia with raspberry tea. They also used it to bring down fevers.

Raspberry was also used to prevent vomiting and was used as a cure for morning sickness in pregnant women. It was used to ease the pains of women in labour and to increase the milk supply of nursing mothers. Diarrhoea was treated with it also.

It was used as a mouthwash for sore gums and mouth

ulcers. Externally it was applied to cuts and sores to accelerate the healing process.

respiratory infections

Cloves were thought to be particularly effective in the treatment of disorders of the respiratory system. Olive oil was also considered to bring relief, as were carrot juice and onion juice.

Turnips were thought to have a beneficial effect on the respiratory system. Nettles were thought to have a similar effect. Sage taken internally at the first symptom of an respiratory infection was meant to be a speedy remedy.

See also ASTHMA; COLDS; COUGHS.

rheumatism

An elder twig carried about the person, according to old folklore, was said to confer protection against rheumatism.

There were several old cures for rheumatism. Two of these involved celery. In one remedy the celery was cut into pieces and boiled in water until it was soft. It was then drunk with water. Another cure involved warming a mixture of boiled celery with milk, nutmeg and a little flour. This was then served with potatoes and pieces of toast.

A drink made from celery was also used as a remedy for rheumatism. Celery seed was boiled in water, reduced, strained, bottled and sealed. This liquid was then taken twice a day for two weeks.

Another cure for rheumatism was based on hot rum. The rum had nutmeg and pepper added to it. This was then drunk by those who were suffering from rheumatic pains.

Wool was used in an external remedy for rheumatism. The wool was heated by holding it against a can containing very hot water as heating it in front of a fire was considered dangerous. This was then applied to the affected joints.

Sometimes a layer of dry, hot wool was wrapped round a painful joint and then the wool was covered with oiled silk. This induced perspiration, and the wool became saturated and had to be changed frequently. This was meant to bring great relief both in rheumatism and gout.

Linseed oil was also used as the basis of a remedy for rheumatism. A lotion was made from linseed oil and oil of turpentine and some spirits of camphor was added. The mixture was then shaken well and the lotion applied to the painful joints.

Garlic, crushed and added to an oil, was applied to painful joints. Raw potato juice and the hot water that potatoes had been boiled in were both also used as external applications. A poultice made from turnip was also used.

Parsley tea, taken internally an hour before meals,

was thought to have the power to stimulate kidney activity and to bring relief to sufferers from rheumatism. Cinnamon taken internally was also thought to relieve the pain of rheumatism, as was watercress or mustard taken internally.

An infusion of burdock was taken to relieve rheumatism. An alternative remedy was an infusion of dock. Meadow-sweet was considered to have an anti-inflammatory action that brought relief to joints made painful by rheumatism.

Diuretics are considered effective in the treatment of rheumatism. In folk medicine, lemon juice and an infusion of dandelion leaves, both being thought to be efficient diuretics, were used as remedies for rheumatism. An infusion of thyme, also thought to be a diuretic, was used too.

rhubarb

In large doses rhubarb was used as a laxative, although in smaller doses it was sometimes used to relieve diarrhoea in infants.

A decoction of the seeds was thought to stimulate the appetite and ease stomach pains.

ringworm

One old cure for ringworm involved putting an application of carbonate of soda and strong vinegar on the affected areas. Another old cure involved cutting the hair from the affected areas and rubbing in turpentine and then washing it off with carbolic soap. The whole head was then to be washed and the areas of ringworm dabbed with diluted iodine.

rose

The Romans used the dog rose to cure anyone who was bitten by a mad dog. Roman women sucked pastilles made of rose to sweeten their breath, and garlands of roses were once worn to prevent drunkenness.

Rose petals were used for the relief of pain in menstruation and were also used to ease heavy bleeding. They were thought to increase fertility and were also thought to have the power to cure impotence in men.

Rose petals were thought to act as a diuretic and were used in disorders of the urinary tract and in disorders of the liver. They were also used as an expectorant. Diarrhoea was treated with rose petals, and roses were used to fight infection in the digestive tract.

Rose-petal tea was used to bring relief to those suffering from colds, catarrh, congestion or influenza. Both the petals and leaves taken in the form of a tea were used to break fevers and induce perspiration.

Depression was treated either with rose petals or rose hips. A syrup made from rose hips was high in vitamin C, as well as other vitamins, and was used to treat the common cold and to raise children's resistance to infection. It was used during and after World War II. The syrup had many uses. It was used to cure stomach cramps, menstrual cramps and diarrhoea. Rose-hip syrup was used as a laxative and as a remedy for nausea, indigestion, and kidney disorders.

A mouthwash and a gargle were made from rose petals, and chapped lips were soothed by rose oil. Rose water was used to clear the skin of blemishes, including acne and spots. Sore eyes were soothed by it, and bruises and sprains were relieved by it. It was thought to have the power to erase wrinkles. Rose water was one of the ingredients in a mouth and throat rinse. The other ingredients were carbolic acid, tincture of orris root, tincture of cala-mus, and nutmeg.

rosemary

Rosemary was believed in early times to keep witches and evil powers at bay. A sprig of it placed under the pillow was thought to have the power to prevent the sleeper from having nightmares, and a sprig worn on the clothing was meant to bring luck and success. It was thought of as being an antidote to the bubonic plague.

Rosemary tea was used to cure headaches, colds and asthma. Colic and flatulence were treated with it. It was used as an expectorant to clear phlegm, and it was used to bring down fevers and induce perspiration.

It was also used as a remedy for nervous disorders and for treating depression. Listlessness was also treated with rosemary.

Rosemary was used to stimulate the circulation and in the treatment of blood pressure, especially low blood pressure. It was also used to stimulate the appetite, to improve brain activity and to increase concentration. The herb was also thought to slow down the ageing process.

Rosemary was to be considered to be a diuretic, and was used as a remedy for arthritis and gout and to improve liver function.

Externally, rosemary oil was used to rub into inflamed joints to relieve the pain and to rub into the temples to cure headaches. Skin infections such as scabies were thought to respond to treatment by an external application of rosemary oil. Bleeding gums were claimed to be cured by a mouthwash made from it, and, when used as a scalp rub, it was thought to prevent hair from falling out.

rowan

The rowan is also known as the mountain ash.

In early folklore rowan was used to keep witches and evil powers at bay.

In folk medicine the berries of the rowan tree were used as a diuretic and as a purgative. They also formed the basis of a gargle for sore throats.

rue

Rue was the subject of several superstitions in folklore. The Romans thought that it conferred the gift of second sight or psychic powers on those who ate it. Musket balls that were soaked in rue water were said always to hit their target. The herb was also used in cursing rituals.

In common with rosemary, rue was thought to be an antidote to the bubonic plague. It was commonly used in treating disorders of the stomach and in relieving muscular cramps. Rue was also used to regulate menstrual disorders.

It was used as a remedy for excessive nervousness and to lower blood pressure.

Rue had to be used with caution as it could bring about abortion and cause allergies of the skin.

S

sage

In Roman times sage juice was thought to be instrumental in helping women to conceive. During the Middle Ages it was regarded as a kind of sovereign cure that could cure just about anything.

It was thought to be a diuretic, and it was also thought to be instrumental in bringing on the menstrual flow and regulating it as well as easing menstrual cramps. The herb was also thought to expel dead foetuses from the womb. It was regarded as being effective in relieving the symptoms of the menopause, particularly hot flushes. Sage was also thought to slow down the ageing process, or even reverse it.

Sage was thought to be effective if it was taken at the first signs of a respiratory infection, and it was used as a treatment for catarrh, sinusitis, bronchitis, asthma and tonsillitis. It was used as a gargle for throat ulcers and as a mouthwash for bleeding gums.

It was used in the treatment of nervous excitement

and other nervous disorders, and it was also thought to be effective in treating some disorders of the stomach. It was used as an aid to digestion and was regarded as a remedy for colic, biliousness and stomach haemorrhages. Dysentery was also treated with it, as was diarrhoea.

Liver complaints were treated with sage. It was regarded as a diuretic and was used as a remedy for gout and arthritis.

Externally, sage tea was applied to heal cuts, wounds, sores, burns, ulcers and insect stings. It was used in a compress in the treatment of strains and to ease sore joints.

salt

Salt is best known as a flavouring for food. In traditional medicine it was commonly used in water to induce vomiting in cases such as poisoning. Such a saline solution was also used as a purgative and was used as an enema to rid children of threadworms. A mixture of salt and water was used in the treatment of catarrh.

A weak solution of salt and water was commonly used as a gargle for sore throats, inflamed gums or mouth ulcers.

savory

Savory is known nowadays as a culinary herb, often used

in salads. However, it was a medicinal herb long before it was used as a culinary herb.

In early times it was a well-known aphrodisiac. Later it was used to stimulate the appetite and to treat stomach complaints. It was also used as a diuretic and as an expectorant.

A gargle was made from it as a cure for sore throats, and it was also used to soothe mouth ulcers.

scabies

Scabies was a very itchy skin condition caused by a parasitic mite.

Watercress applied in a poultice was used in the treatment of scabies. Dilute rosemary oil rubbed on the skin was also thought to help. A more unusual-sounding cure was the application of baked apple to the skin to ease scabies.

An old method of soothing the itchy skin in scabies involved applying a weak solution of vinegar to the skin. Another remedy was a weak solution of carbolic acid, while yet another was a solution of bicarbonate of soda.

Rubbing soft soap all over the body, taking a hot bath, and scrubbing the body all over with a nail brush were parts of another suggested remedy. After this, the skin was dried and sulphur ointment was rubbed in and not washed off for twelve hours. Any clothes that had been worn by the scabies sufferer had to be baked.

scalds *see* **burns and scalds**.

scarlet fever

Pepper was an old folk remedy for scarlet fever. A weak solution of vinegar and water was also thought to relieve the condition. Eucalyptus, which was thought to have antiseptic properties and which was also thought to bring down fevers, was also used in the treatment of scarlet fever.

sciatica

An old cure for sciatica involved burning bean husks to ashes. These were added to unsalted lard and mixed to make an ointment. It was then applied to the areas affected by the sciatica. Stinging the skin of the part affected by sciatica with nettles was thought to bring some relief by acting as a counterirritant and so increasing the flow of blood to the skin.

Dilute chamomile oil massaged into the painful joints was supposed to bring relief to sufferers from sciatica.

Eggs were once thought to relieve the nerve pain of sciatica. Elderberries taken internally were also thought to be a remedy.

Herbs used as remedies for sciatica included broom, ground elder, ground ivy, kidneywort, St John's wort and wintergreen.

seasickness

It was advocated that whoever was embarking on a voyage should eat well before setting out on the journey. At least this avoided the singular unpleasantness of retching on an empty stomach.

If sickness occurred despite sailing on a full stomach and the sickness was prolonged, it was suggested that the person suffering from seasickness should swallow the raw white of an egg beaten in cold water. If this stayed down it was to be followed by a whole raw egg mixed with a little brandy.

See also NAUSEA; VOMITING.

self-heal

Self-heal was also known as sicklewort. As its name suggests, its medicinal properties have long been recognized.

It was taken internally as a treatment for diphtheria and was noted for its use as a remedy for sore throats. It was also used as a tonic and for the cure of internal bleeding.

Externally it was used to treat sore throats, mouth ulcers and burns.

shepherd's purse

Shepherd's purse was used in the treatment of kidney disorders and as a remedy for low blood pressure. It was also used to stimulate the menstrual flow and to stop nosebleeds and heal wounds when taken internally. Diarrhoea was treated with it.

Externally, shepherd's purse was used to reduce inflammation in chilblains.

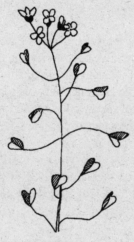

shepherd's purse

shingles

A poultice of cabbage leaves was applied to the skin to effect relief in shingles. Balm was also used externally in the treatment of the illness.

sinusitis

Onions taken internally were considered to be an effective cure for sinusitis. Watercress, also taken internally, was thought to bring relief, as was plantain. Elderflowers, with their supposed decongestant properties, and a decoction of eucalyptus leaves, also with supposed decongestant properties, were held to be remedies for sinusitis.

Sage taken at the start of any sign of infection was thought to be curative. Both honey and tea were thought to be beneficial in the treatment of sinusitis.

Thyme oil, used as an inhalant, was considered to bring about the relief of sinusitis. Chamomile oil was also used in this way to the same effect.

skin problems

Many herbs were frequently used in the treatment of skin complaints. These included avens, betony, borage and burdock. Butterbur, chamomile, catnip and chervil were also used.

Other herbs that were used included chickweed, coltsfoot, comfrey, dandelion, dock, fenugreek, flax, groundsel and hawthorn. Herb robert, kidneywort, lady's bedstraw, lavender, lime flowers, meadowsweet and madder were also used. Nettle, pansy, peppermint, plantain, primrose, raspberry were used in skin complaints, as were rosemary, sage, slippery elm, sorrel, speedwell, tansy, watercress, white horehound and witch hazel.

Cinnamon was also used externally, as were lemon, raw potato juice, vinegar, carrot and turnip.

skullcap

In the eighteenth century herbalists recommended the use of skullcap as a treatment for anyone who had been bitten by a dog that was thought to be rabid. For this reason the plant was sometimes known as mad dog. Its common name of skullcap is thought to refer to the fact that it was once used in the treatment of mental patients.

Skullcap was used as a remedy for nervous disorders, including nervous tremors and hysteria. It was also used as a remedy for lockjaw and convulsions and muscular spasms. High blood pressure was treated with it.

It had to be used with caution as it was liable to cause drowsiness, and indeed it was used as a cure for insomnia.

sleeplessness *see* insomnia

slippery elm

Slippery elm is also known as red elm or sweet elm.

It was the moist inner bark of the tree that was used medicinally, hence its name. Taken internally, it was used as a laxative or as a means of easing the process of childbirth. Externally it was used in the treatment of boils.

smallpox

Pepper was an old remedy for smallpox. Meadowsweet was also once used in the treatment of the disease.

It was also treated with a drink consisting of a teaspoonful of cream of tartar and half a pint of hot water.

An unpleasant remedy involved administering fried mice to the patient, it being thought preferable for the mice to be fried alive.

snake bites

Peppermint was used by the Greeks and Romans to cure snake bites.

A common remedy was to tie a ligature above the wound and suck it. The wound was to be encouraged to bleed and was to be washed in ammonia or tincture of iodine. Sal volatile was to be given to the person who had been bitten as a treatment and to keep the person awake.

A far more drastic treatment involved the filling of the wound with gunpowder and blood. The paste was then ignited to cauterize it thoroughly.

sore throats *see* throats, sore.

sorrel

Sorrel is also known as green sorrel and cuckoo sorrow. It was used in feverish illnesses as a cooling drink. A mixture of sorrel juice and vinegar was given as a remedy for ringworm. A decoction of sorrel was said to cure jaundice and kidney stones. It was also used for haemorrhages.

southernwood

Southernwood is also known as old man and lad's love. It is called lad's love because it was once thought to be an aphrodisiac.

It is a very strong-smelling herb and was once used as an insect repellent. Because the smell was so strong it was carried by some people to disguise nastier smells.

The herb was used in cases of menstrual irregularities, especially to encourage the menstrual flow. It was used as a general antiseptic.

snapdragon

According to folklore, snapdragon was used to keep witches and evil powers at bay.

The fresh leaves applied as a poultice were used in the treatment of ulcers and tumours.

spearmint

Spearmint was used in some remedies to take away the unpleasant tastes of the other herbs used in them.

It was used as an aid to digestion and as a remedy for indigestion, flatulence and cramp. Headaches and colds were also treated with it.

speedwell

Speedwell is also known as cat's eye, bird's eye and gipsyweed.

In folk medicine it was used in the treatment of skin diseases. Stomach disorders were also treated by it, and it was used as a diuretic. Bronchitis and other respiratory problems were treated with it.

spitting of blood

The spitting up of blood was thought to be cured by drinking sage tea sweetened with honey.

Plantain, taken internally, was also thought to stop the bleeding. An unpleasant cure involving plantain was once thought to be an effective remedy. The juice of plantain was mixed with mice droppings that had been ground to a powder. This was to be taken before going to sleep at night and in the morning before breakfast.

sprains

There are several traditional cures for sprains. Bathing with vinegar was said to be effective, as was rubbing the sprain with a liniment made from olive oil and grated garlic. Rose water, lavender oil and witch hazel were used to reduce swelling, while an older cure involved applying the beaten white of an egg to the sprained area.

Comfrey was noted for its healing powers, and a poultice of comfrey was used on sprains. Plantain was also noted as an effective wound healer, and its crushed fresh leaves were used on sprained ankles and other sprains.

Plantain was also used as one of the ingredients in a more complex remedy. The leaves of elder, ground ivy, wormwood and plantain were chopped and mixed with lard. The mixture was then put in a slow oven until the leaves were crisp and then the mixture was strained through linen.

Another cure for sprains involved warming three parts elder leaves to four parts lard and two parts grated suet. After the lard mixture had turned green, it was strained through linen before being applied to the sprain.

The leaves of tansy were also thought to relieve sprains. These were applied in the form of a poultice.

stiffness

A remedy for stiffness occurring after exercise involved soaking in the hottest bath that could be tolerated for at least ten minutes. Then a little camphorated oil was rubbed on the skin and kneaded into the muscles Then salicylate of soda was taken in a glass of water before going to bed.

stings and bites

The Romans used peppermint to bring relief to insect bites and stings. Later a whole variety of natural substances were used in folk medicine for this purpose.

stings

The crushed fresh leaves of several plants were used to rub on the affected part. These included parsley, plantain and balm. The leaves or flowers of marigold could be crushed and applied to the bite or sting. The leaf of the broad-leaved dock was a traditional remedy for nettle stings, dock handily often being found where nettles grow.

Crushed garlic or garlic macerated in oil was rubbed on insect bites and stings, and a cut leek could also be used for this. Onion juice was rubbed on animal bites.

Sage tea applied to bites and stings was also thought to bring relief, as was a poultice made with cabbage. Cinnamon, oil of cardamom and oil of lavender were also used. Vinegar and witch hazel were another two possible remedies.

In the case of the stinge of bees, wasps and hornets, it was advised to extract the sting and to apply ammonia or bicarbonate of soda. These were also recommended for the bites of ants, gnats and mosquitoes.

Another cure for bee stings was to remove the sting and then put a cold compress on it, followed by a hot compress. An alternative remedy was to cover the affected area with damp, cold soil.

Yet another cure for bee stings involved rubbing a little olive oil on the affected area. If this did not work, a poultice was to be applied. Honey applied to an area stung by a bee was thought to be effective.

St Jacob's oil was recommended in one cure for

hornet stings. One cure recommended for anyone bitten by an adder was more complicated. It involved taking nine cloves of garlic and peeling them carefully. A spoonful of treacle and two pints of new strong ale were then added and mixed well. The patient was encouraged to drink freely of this mixture. He or she was to be well wrapped up while taking the cure to encourage perspiration.

stitch

One old cure for a stitch in the side involved applying to the affected side a mixture of treacle mixed with very hot potato.

Treacle was also used in a more complicated and less pleasant cure. A gallon of new ale was mixed with as much of the dung of a stallion as would make a thick mixture. A pound of treacle, some sliced ginger and some saffron were then added. It was then put in a cold still before the mixture was administered, three or four spoonfuls at a time, to the person suffering from the stitch.

St John's wort

St John's wort is also known as fairy herb.

In folklore the herb was used to keep at bay witches, ghosts and demons. It was also thought to have the power to protect a house from lightning.

Early herbalists used St John's wort in the treatment

of insanity and melancholy. It was later used against hysteria.

It was used in the treatment of haemorrhages and in the spitting up of blood. Intestinal worms were treated with it, and it was given to children to stop them from bed-wetting.

Externally it was used to treat skin irritations and bruising. It was also used to soothe engorged breasts in nursing mothers.

St John's wort

stomach pains

The application of heat has long been thought to have a therapeutic effect on abdominal pain or cramps. Hot fomentations were once recommended. This involved pouring boiling water over a piece of flannel or other cloth, wringing the cloth out to get rid of as much water as possible and applying it to the area to be treated, in this case the abdomen. The hot cloths had to be replaced as soon as they began to get cool, and it was recommended that a piece of flannel or a pad of cotton wool was placed over the treated area to prevent a chill. Hot bran was sometimes used as a somewhat messier alternative.

Heat is still thought to be therapeutic in cases of abdominal pain, or at least known to be a source of comfort to the sufferer. Nowadays, however, it is usually applied in a more efficient manner, the patient clutching a hot-water bottle to the abdominal area or soaking in a hot bath.

Peppermint was thought to be instrumental in curing abdominal pain and spasm. Parsley, thyme, sage, cloves, chamomile and meadowsweet were thought of as cures in that they reduced spasm.

Various suggested remedies involving some kind of potion have been suggested over the centuries for this painful common disorder. In one of these remedies a pint of milk was heated and given to the patient after four tablespoons of brandy had been added to it.

Another involved boiling a handful of betony in white wine, straining this and giving it to the patient to drink. A hot drink containing cinnamon is another traditional remedy, and a mixture using parsley seeds was sometimes administered.

stomach problems

A traditional charm to keep abdominal pain and colic at bay was a hare's foot with the joint still in it. One of the people who believed that carrying such a charm would keep him pain-free and flatulence-free was the seventeenth-century diarist Samuel Pepys.

stomach problems

Many herbs were used in the treatment of stomach complaints. These included angelica, basil, caraway, centaury, chicory, comfrey, fennel, garlic and groundsel. Kidney-wort, knotgrass, marigold, marjoram and meadowsweet were also used as remedies for stomach problems, as were rue, slippery elm, speedwell and tarragon.

stones

Strawberries were used as an old cure for gallstones. A mixture of olive oil and lemon juice was also thought to help. The juice of raw potato was also used, as were dandelion and peppermint.

Herbs that were considered to be effective included barberry, chicory, knotgrass and madder.

strains

Strains were treated with vinegar, and witch hazel was a popular remedy. Sage tea was also used either in the form of a compress or in the form of a liniment. A poultice or ointment made with comfrey was also used to relieve strains.

strawberry

Strawberry has long been used for medicinal purposes.

It was used to treat anaemia and to lower high blood pressure. Strawberry was also used in the treatment of stomach complaints, as a tonic and as a laxative. Intestinal worms were thought to be expelled by eating strawberries. The leaves were used to treat dysentery and the root was thought to be a remedy for diarrhoea.

Kidney complaints were also treated with it, as were gallstones. It was used as a diuretic, and gout was treated by it.

Externally, it was used cosmetically to improve the complexion. A cut strawberry rubbed on sunburn was meant to relieve it.

styes *see* **eye problems**.

sulphur

Sulphur was used in various folk cures.

It was used in the relief of croup. A mixture consisting of a teaspoonful of sulphur, a teaspoonful of vinegar and the beaten white of an egg was administered to the patient.

Itch was also treated with it. Sulphur baths were recommended in such skin conditions as ringworm.

Sulphur was also used in a treatment for dandruff. It

was mixed with water and the mixture shaken thoroughly several times. The scalp and hair were then saturated with it.

sunburn

A cut strawberry rubbed on an area of sunburn was thought to bring relief. Grated potato mixed with olive oil was also thought to relieve sunburn. Vinegar rubbed on the skin was also used to treat sunburn.

Cucumber juice was used to cool sunburn, and it was sometimes mixed with rose water. Crushed marigolds were also used to ease sunburn, as was glycerine, sometimes mixed with rose water. Washing the sunburn in sage tea was another suggested remedy.

Egg white applied to the skin in layers with time being allowed for each layer to dry before the other layer was applied was considered to soothe sunburn. Buttermilk was also supposed to ease the pain of sunburn.

An old cure for sunburn involved mixing cream, lemon, brandy, alum and sugar. This was boiled, skimmed, cooled and applied to the skin.

Another old cure was based on grapes. A bunch of green grapes was sprinkled with a mixture of salt and powdered alum. The grapes were wrapped in paper and baked. The juice was squeezed out of the grapes and was then applied to the area of skin suffering from sunburn.

Lemon juice applied to the skin was meant to prevent sunburn.

sunstroke

An old method of preventing sunstroke was to wear a cabbage leaf inside the crown of a hat.

If someone was suffering from bad sunstroke it was recommended that the person's clothing should be loosened and cold water poured over him or her. Alternatively, clothing was to be removed and the patient covered with a sheet that had to be kept drenched with cold water.

Another cure involved the application of mustard leaves to the nape of the neck of the person suffering from sunstroke.

T

tansy

Tansy is also known as wormwort because it was frequently used to get rid of worms, especially in children. In ancient times it was spread on corpses or else bunches were put in the shrouds of the dead to keep away maggots. It was also rubbed on meat to keep flies away.

Although extensively used to get rid of worms, it had to be used with caution as in extreme doses it was violently irritant. It was used as an aid to digestion and as a treatment for nausea. Nervous disorders and hysteria were also treated with it, as was epilepsy. Menstrual problems were treated with it, as it was used to bring on menstrual bleeding.

Externally it was used as a treatment for bruises and some disorders of the skin. It was used as a remedy for sprains and to reduce swelling.

tapeworm

An old cure for tapeworm involved taking a solution of

salt one evening and a draught of bitter aloes the next morning.

One suggested method of curing tapeworm seems less likely to work. It involved the person who was unlucky enough to have the tapeworm having to fast for three or four days. After that he or she had to endure the spectacle of having a steak cooked in front of him or her. Supposedly the tapeworm was so hungry by this stage that it leapt out of the patient's mouth in order to get to the food.

tarragon

Tarragon is also known as French tarragon. We now know tarragon as a culinary herb but it was used in herbal medicine also.

It was used mainly as a remedy for disorders connected with the digestive system. It was used as an aid to digestion and to stimulate the appetite. Nausea, indigestion and flatulence were all treated with it.

tea

Tea has been used in Chinese medicine for thousands of years and was used by the ancient Greeks for bronchitis, asthma and colds.

It was thought to stimulate the system generally, reduce fatigue and bring about a feeling of wellbeing. It was thought to improve circulation and was used as a relaxant in asthma. Catarrh and sinusitis were treated with it. It was used as a diuretic and as a treatment for diarrhoea. It was also thought to confer some protection against heart disease and to retard the ageing process.

Used externally, cold tea was an old remedy for burns and scalds, and it was also used in the treatment of external ulcers. It was used to stop or decrease bleeding, and this property made it useful as a remedy for bleeding gums.

Again externally, it was used as a remedy for swollen eyes. It was also used to make a mouthwash for ulcers.

Herbal teas are now very popular with people who wish to avoid the caffeine in tea or coffee, or with people who just like the taste of them and find them refreshing. A large range of them is available commercially.

Herbal teas, however, were once used more for medicinal purposes than for refreshment. They were used as a remedy for various conditions, according to the herb involved. There were a great many of them and they included:

balm tea, also known as *lemon balm tea*, which was thought to be a restorative and stimulant. It was given by mothers to their children to give them energy.

chamomile tea, which was used to induce a calming effect. Taken before retiring, it was used as a remedy for insomnia. It was also used as a stimulant of the appetite, as an aid to digestion and as a remedy for flatulence and indigestion.

comfrey tea, which was used as a remedy for anaemia, asthma and gastric ulcers.

elderflower tea, which was recommended to be taken at the onset of the symptoms of a cold. It was thought to induce perspiration and so speed the cure.

hawthorn tea, which was thought to be health-giving. It was thought to be particularly beneficial for people who were of a nervous disposition.

linseed tea, which was made from flax and liquorice root. It was used as a remedy for coughs.

motherwort tea, which was used as a stimulant for tired brains and was taken to improve concentration.

parsley tea, which was thought to stimulate the action of the kidneys if it was drunk in significant quantities before meals. It was thought to be an effective cure for rheumatism.

peppermint tea, which was recommended as a bedtime drink to cure a cold, especially if it had honey added to it. It was also used as cure for flatulence and nausea.

sage tea, which was taken to get rid of infections. It was taken to cure infections of the respiratory system and was thought to be particularly effective as a cure for sore throats. As well as sage, rosemary, honeysuckle and plantain were sometimes added to make the tea, and it was sweetened with honey.

Externally it was used as a gargle and as a hair wash.

strawberry tea, which was said to be an effective remedy for cases of gout and was also used as a treatment for kidney problems. It was also used to treat intestinal worms.

thyme tea, which was used as a remedy for chest disorders and for sore throats.

yarrow tea, which was recommended as bedtime drink in cases of bad colds. Yarrow leaves were often used in conjunction with elderflowers to make yarrow tea.

Sometimes a kind of tea was made from meat as well as herbs. Beef tea, for example, described under BEEF TEA, and chicken tea were both used as a pick-me-up for invalids or people who were convalescing after an illness.

teething

Dill water was often given to children when they were teething, especially when the teething seemed to be causing colic or flatulence. Magnesia was sometimes added to the dill water.

thistle, holy

Holy thistle is also known as blessed thistle.

It was used to treat weak stomachs to act as a stimulant of the appetite and to prevent nausea, although taken in large doses it was also used to induce vomiting. Holy thistle was also used to expel intestinal worms.

The herb was used also to purify the blood and to

improve circulation. Feverish conditions were treated with it.

It was used to bring on the menstrual flow and to increase the milk supply in nursing mothers.

throats, sore

There were several old cures for sore throats. Some of these were stranger than others.

In one rather weird cure a piece of raw bacon was tied to a length of strong cotton. The person suffering from the sore throat had to swallow the bacon while holding tightly to the cotton. The fat was then pulled back up by the cotton and this exercise was repeated half a dozen times. A black cashmere stocking that had been worn for a week then had the sole of it sprinkled with eucalyptus. This was placed against the throat and the rest of the stocking wrapped around the neck and pinned. The patient then retired for the night.

Another old cure involved filling a stocking or large sock with cooking salt, which was sometimes heated first. The sock or stocking was wound round the neck of the person with the sore throat before he or she retired for the night.

There were several other more ordinary-sounding cures. Some camphor was added to a wineglass of brandy. This mixture was poured over a lump of loaf sugar. The sugar lump was allowed to dissolve in the mouth of the person who was suffering from the sore throat. This was repeated every hour until four doses had been taken. After this the sore throat was confidently predicted to have disappeared.

An infusion of elderberries sweetened with honey sipped slowly was a suggested remedy. An infusion of yarrow root taken three times a day was also supposed to bring relief. Eating onions boiled in molasses was supposed to be particularly effective if the sore throat was accompanied by hoarseness.

A weak solution of salt was used as a gargle to bring relief to sore throats, as were a mixture of lemon juice and warm water, and a dilute mixture of iodine and water. A little vinegar added to water was also used as a gargle, as was an infusion of mustard.

An infusion of sage leaves with added vinegar and a little honey was used as a gargle. Other gargles included barley water, sage tea, borage tea, dock, peppermint, eucalyptus oil, witch hazel and myrrh. Hot vinegar was used as an inhalation.

Garlic juice taken internally was thought to help. Eating leeks was also used as a remedy, as was eating onions. A hot tea made from rosemary was also used in the treatment of sore throats, and comfrey was a popular remedy taken internally. A hot infusion of yarrow was also taken for the relief of sore throats.

thyme

In folklore it was thought that an elixir including thyme would give those who drank it the power to see fairies.

In herbal medicine, thyme was used as an antiseptic. In the treatment of bronchitis it was used as an expectorant, and asthma, whooping cough, pleurisy and pneumonia and colds were treated with it. It was thought to be a remedy for sore throats. Thyme was sometimes used in conjunction with cinnamon in the treatment of bronchial conditions. It was also sometimes mixed with honey.

An antispasmodic, it was used in the treatment of colic and flatulence. It was used as an aid to digestion and to stimulate the appetite. Dysentery and diarrhoea were treated with it.

It was a diuretic and was used in gout and urinary tract infections. Nervous disorders were treated with it, it being used to allay anxiety and to cure insomnia and depression.

Externally it was used to treat insect bites and to relieve muscular pains. It was used as an inhalant in the treatment of colds, catarrh, sinusitis and asthma and to make a mouthwash and gargle for sore throats.

toothache

According to old folklore, prevention was better than

cure as far as toothache is concerned. Several charms were suggested to ward off toothache. One rather macabre charm against toothache was a tooth taken from a corpse and worn round the neck. A double nut carried in the pocket was also supposed to keep toothache at bay.

People who were unlucky enough to get toothache were even more unlucky when they were subjected to some of the stranger early cures. None of the old English cures was, however, quite as bad as an ancient Egyptian cure that involved applying the body of a freshly killed mouse to the aching tooth.

A Welsh cure for toothache came close to the Egyptian one in terms of unpleasantness. This involved pounding lizards and fern beetles in an iron pot and making a powder from them. The wet forefinger was then dipped in the powder and applied to the tooth frequently until the tooth supposedly painlessly came out.

Another remedy was not so gruesome. It involved the person suffering from toothache lying on the opposite side of the body from the side where the toothache was. Three drops of rue juice were then dropped into the ear on the same side as the aching tooth. It was allowed to remain for an hour or two, after which the toothache was supposed to have disappeared.

Whisky was involved in at least two cures. In one, a piece of cotton wadding or cotton wool moistened with whisky was placed on the tooth. In another, a small piece of strong brown paper was dipped in whisky, sprinkled with pepper and applied to the face at the point where the aching tooth was. This was covered with a flannel bandage and left until a cure was effected.

A piece of cloth dipped in a mixture of creosote, brandy and sweet spirits of nitre was held to be curative. Alternatively, a little bryonia liniment was added to warm water. This mixture was added to a glass of warm water and held in the mouth over the tooth that was giving problems.

Fresh ginger was chewed to dull the pain of toothache. Ginger was also used as an internal cure. Ground ginger was mixed with Epsom salts and added to hot water.

Cinnamon oil applied directly to the tooth was thought to bring relief to toothache while a piece of cotton wool soaked in oil of cloves applied in the same way was a common popular cure. Peppermint oil was also used to ease toothache. Onion juice was also put on cotton wool and applied to the aching tooth, as was the juice of fresh parsley.

An infusion of watercress was used as a mouthwash for toothache, and chewing fresh yarrow leaves was another suggested cure. Chamomile taken internally was also thought to be helpful.

Herbs thought to be effective in the curing of toothache,

apart from those already mentioned, included broom, lavender, marjoram and wintergreen.

tuberculosis

Tuberculosis is more commonly known as TB and was formerly commonly known as consumption.

Raw eggs or lightly cooked eggs were used in the diet of people suffering from tuberculosis as they were meant to build up the strength of the invalids.

Turnip juice was given as part of the treatment of tuberculosis. Carrots were another remedy for the condition. Myrrh, which was thought to be an expectorant and decongestant, was also used as a remedy for TB.

turnip

Turnip was known in folk medicine as a purifier of the blood. Being rich in vitamin C, it was used to treat scurvy and was thought to give clear skins to people who ate it regularly. It was also used to increase energy and cure depression.

Turnips were also used in disorders of the urinary tract, being used as a diuretic and to cure kidney stones. Gout and arthritis were treated with them. They were used as a remedy for bronchitis, and the juice was used in the treatment of tuberculosis. Turnip juice was also used as a decongestant in colds, catarrh and coughs.

Externally turnips were used in poultices as a remedy

for boils, abscesses and chilblains. Swollen joints in arthritis, gout and rheumatism were said to be helped by the application of a turnip poultice.

typhoid fever

Honey was used as a antiseptic in the treatment of typhoid. Garlic was also used, and eucalyptus was another old remedy.

typhus

Pepper was an old remedy for infections such as typhus. Vinegar was also used because of its antiseptic properties. Typhus was also treated with garlic.

U

ulcers, external

One cure for ulcers on the skin involved bruising primrose leaves with the same quantity of primrose flowers and simmering them in unsalted lard until the primroses were crisp. The mixture was then strained, allowed to cool and applied to the ulcer.

Another cure was based on carrots. These were grated, made into a poultice and applied directly to the ulcer. A poultice based on watercress was also used, and cabbage leaves were also used in the form of a poultice. A burdock poultice, or a comfrey poultice, was also advocated.

Honey was used externally as a remedy for ulcers, as was the juice of raw potato. A lotion made from cold tea was also considered to be effective against ulcers, as was a lotion made from an infusion of dandelion leaves and flowers. Dilute chamomile oil and dilute lavender oil were other remedies recommended for ulcers on the skin, and eucalyptus oil was also used externally. Ulcers were also treated with sage tea.

Crushed marigold flowers or an infusion of marigold were also used externally to heal ulcers. Yarrow, elder-flowers and borage were also used in this way.

ulcers, internal

Honey taken in boiled water was a remedy for throat ulcers. Throat ulceration was also treated with a mixture of powdered alum, whites of egg and tincture of camphor. A weak solution of salt was used as a remedy for mouth ulcers, and sage tea was used for this condition too.

Mouthwashes made either from dock or meadowsweet were recommended for mouth ulcers.

Peptic ulcers were treated with raw potato juice, apples or carrots. Olive oil and balm were both thought to soothe them, and chamomile, meadowsweet and marigold were all used to heal them. An infusion of comfrey leaves was thought to be beneficial in the treatment of gastric ulcers and duodenal ulcers.

urinary disorders

Dandelions were a popular remedy for urinary disorders, and cloves were also thought to be beneficial. Leeks and onions were considered to be an effective cure also, as were plantain and comfrey.

Balm, thyme and eucalyptus were all used as remedies, and a tea made from linseed and lemon was also recommended.

V

valerian

Valerian is also known as all-heal.

In early folklore valerian was thought to have aphrodisiac properties and to be an aid to psychic powers. Rats seemed to be attracted to it, and it has been suggested that the Pied Piper of Hamelin was carrying sprigs of valerian when he persuaded the rats to follow him.

Its main use was as a sedative and tranquillizer to treat nervous disorders. It was also used to reduce hyperactivity and to cure insomnia. It was thought to relieve pain.

Valerian was used in epilepsy as an anti-convulsant. Oil of valerian was used as a treatment for cholera and to strengthen eyesight.

varicose veins

A poultice of comfrey was used in the treatment of varicose veins. Marigold was also used, either in the form of an infusion or in the form of crushed fresh flowers, as was yarrow. A poultice or compress made with witch hazel was also used for varicose veins to lessen the pain.

valerian

vertigo *see* **dizziness**.

vervain
Vervain is also known as herb of grace.

vervain

In early folklore, superstitions endowed vervain with various powers. It was supposed to be able to open locked doors. If a piece was hung around the neck it kept bad dreams at bay. As a supposed aphrodisiac it was used in love potions.

Medically it was regarded as an antidote to poisons and the bites of mad dogs and snakes. Early herbalists used it to cleanse the body of impurities.

Vervain was recommended as a treatment for nervous disorders and for hysteria. It was thought to raise the spirits of people who were suffering from depression.

Anaemia was treated with it, as were ulcers, pleurisy and intermittent fevers. As an antispasmodic it was used to reduce muscular spasm in some disorders. It was also used to treat eye disorders and to improve the supply of milk in nursing mothers.

Externally it was used in poultices as a remedy for earache, headaches and rheumatism. Also externally, it was used as a remedy for haemorrhoids.

vinegar

Vinegar had several uses in folk medicine. It was used from early times as a remedy for disorders of the respiratory system, such as catarrh. It was also used to bring down fevers and as a gargle for the relief of sore throats and laryngitis.

Vinegar was also used in the treatment of urinary infections such as cystitis. In addition, taken with water, it was an old antiseptic remedy for such diseases as scarlet fever, dysentery and typhus.

It was an old folk cure for wounds as it was thought to

221

speed up the healing process, stop bleeding and reduce inflammation and swelling. An application of
vinegar was thought to relieve sprains, bruises, and
stings.

Eczema and similar skin conditions and rashes were
treated with it, and it was also thought to be an effective remedy for ringworm and athlete's foot. Sunburn
was treated with vinegar, sometimes with rose petals
soaked in it. People suffering from headaches often
sponged their foreheads with vinegar.

violet

Violet is also called sweet violet.

Violet was used for treating bronchitis, catarrh and
asthma. It was also used as diuretic and a laxative.

Violet was used in the treatment of ague, epilepsy,
pleurisy and jaundice. Insomnia was also treated by it,
and it was also used as a painkiller. In the early years of
this century it was used against cancer.

vomiting

Honey was a popular cure for vomiting as it was for
several other diseases. An infusion of eucalyptus leaves
was also used, as was a hot infusion of cardamom
seeds.

Water was recommended during bouts of vomiting
as it prevents dehydration.

Salt was used to induce vomiting, as was mustard. A mixture of salt and vinegar was sometimes used to induce vomiting, as in cases of poisoning.

See also NAUSEA.

W

walnut

The bark and leaves of walnut were used in the treatment of skin conditions, such as eczema, and in the healing of ulcers. An infusion of the bark was used as a purgative, and green walnuts were used to expel worms.

The vinegar in which walnuts were pickled was used as a remedy for sore throats.

warts

Onion juice was suggested as a cure for warts, as were dandelion juice, leek juice, mullein juice, rue juice and the juice of St John's wort. An infusion of marigold, or the crushed fresh flowers of marigold, was used also as a remedy, and the warts were also rubbed night and morning with cinnamon oil in an attempt to get rid of them. Another recommended remedy was the rubbing of the warts with a raw potato, and yet another involved rubbing the warts with castor oil.

Thyme juice boiled with pepper in wine and the juice

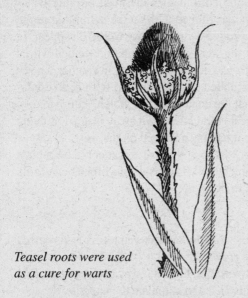

*Teasel roots were used
as a cure for warts*

of teasel roots boiled in wine were both regarded as remedies. The juice of wheat ears was mixed with salt to form another cure for warts, and willow bark was burnt and its ashes mixed with vinegar to be applied as lotion to the warts.

A more curious cure involved tying a horse hair round the individual warts and applying spider webs, pig's blood or the juice from ants. Rubbing the wart with the blood of eels was another suggested old remedy.

225

Several supposed remedies involved burying whatever the wart was rubbed with, in the belief that as the buried object rotted away the wart would disappear. In one of these the wart was cut open and rubbed with a sour apple that was afterwards buried. In another, a piece of meat was rubbed on the wart and buried, a stipulation being that the meat had to be stolen. Alternatively, the stolen meat could be thrown away instead of being buried when it had been rubbed on the wart.

Raw bacon was something else that could be rubbed on the wart and buried. The inside of a broad bean could also be used in this way.

watercress

Early herbalists recommended watercress as a remedy for poor hair growth.

Because it was high in iron it was used to treat anaemia. It was also used to stimulate the appetite.

An expectorant, it was used as a remedy in the treatment of bronchitis and asthma. As a diuretic, it was used in the treatment of urinary disorders. Disorders of the liver and gall bladder were treated with it.

Watercress was also used in nervous disorders.

It was used to stimulate menstruation and increase the milk supply in nursing mothers. It was also thought to increase fertility.

Externally, watercress was used in the form of a

poultice to treat wounds, boils, ulcers, cold sores and scabies. It was also used to make a lotion for haemorrhoids and rashes. A mouthwash made from it was used for the relief of toothache.

water retention *see* **diuretics**.

weakness *see* **debility**.

white bryony
White bryony is sometimes known as bryony or English

white bryony

mandrake. It was popularly regarded as having aphrodisiac powers and was considered by the Romans to afford protection against lightning.

It was a plant that had to be used with extreme caution. The dried root was used in some folk remedies, but it is toxic and could induce vomiting and gastric pain. The berries are also poisonous.

It was used as purgative and in diseases of the respiratory system, such as bronchitis, pneumonia, influenza and coughs. Heart disorders caused by gout or rheumatism and malaria were also treated with it.

whooping cough

Thyme was thought to have properties that could relieve whooping cough, while an infusion of garlic rubbed on the chest was also thought to bring relief to the sufferer. Oil of cloves, sometimes combined with olive oil, was also rubbed on the chest.

Eucalyptus was used in the form of a decoction of the leaves taken internally. The oil was also put in very hot water and used as an inhalation.

Another remedy involved filling a kettle as full as possible, boiling it, adding a spoonful of carbolic acid and letting the steam fill the room. This was supposed to relieve the symptoms of whooping cough.

A mixture of ground alum and powdered sugar was

recommended to be taken by the sufferer several times a day. Another mixture that was used as a remedy consisted of West Indian rum, aniseed oil and lemon juice.

There were some extremely odd old cures for whooping cough. One particularly unpleasant one involved holding a frog or toad for a few moments with its head in the mouth of the sufferer. Sometimes a fish was put into the patient's mouth and then thrown into a river, the idea being that it would take the whooping cough infection into the water with it.

A mixture of crushed wood lice and breast milk from a nursing mother taken every morning for several days was another cure and probably one that did not appeal very much to the person forced to take it. He or she would probably have preferred another cure, which involved passing the patient three times under the belly of a donkey and then passing him or her three times over the back of a donkey.

willow, white
The bark and leaves of the white willow were used in herbal medicine. The bark was used to reduce fevers in some conditions and as a remedy for indigestion, dysentery, diarrhoea and worms. It was used as a tonic for people recovering from illness.

wind *see* flatulence.

wintergreen

Oil of wintergreen was used to soothe pain, including that caused by rheumatism and arthritis. It was also used to treat bruises.

Taken internally wintergreen was used as a gargle.

witch hazel

Witch hazel was used to stop both internal and external bleeding, and in the treating of haemorrhoids and heavy menstrual bleeding. It was also used to treat diarrhoea and dysentery, venereal disease and tuberculosis.

However, its principal use was as an external remedy for bruises, sprains and inflammation. It was used also to treat burns, bites and stings, and varicose veins.

woodruff

Woodruff was used as a diuretic and was a remedy for some disorders of the kidneys and liver. It was also used as a tonic and as a treatment for some heart disorders. Stomach pains were also treated by it.

Because of its fragrance it was used in the Middle Ages to freshen rooms. It was hung in bundles in houses.

worms

One pleasant cure for intestinal worms involved eating strawberries. Garlic was a popular cure, and lemon was also thought to be instrumental in getting rid of worms.

A tincture of thyme taken before eating in the morning or an infusion of nettles were also advocated as remedies.

Eating potato salad with walnut oil for several days in succession was an old suggested remedy for worms. Cucumber seeds was another remedy that was advocated.

Other plants that were used to expel worms included aloes, primrose and walnuts.

Enemas were frequently given to children to get rid of thread worms. One enema consisted of salt and water.

wormwood

As the name suggests, wormwood was used to expel worms from the intestines. Early herbalists used wormwood as a diuretic and as an antidote to poison.

It was also used as an antiseptic and as a stimulant of the appetite.

wounds

Herbs that were used to heal wounds include adder's tongue, arnica, burdock, comfrey, dock, knotgrass, myrrh, parsley, plantain, sage and yarrow.

Honey, potatoes, pepper and apples mixed with olive oil were used in the dressing and healing of wounds. Tea was used to check bleeding of wounds, as were nettles. Cloves and cinnamon were also recommended to help in the healing process of wounds. Lavender was used to clean wounds, and borage tea was used to speed the healing process. Witch hazel was a popular cure.

Vinegar was a old remedy for wounds. In the nursery rhyme 'Jack and Jill', Jack has his head dressed with vinegar and brown paper when he 'breaks his crown'.

Poultices made from cabbage and from carrots were also used as folk remedies for wounds. The leaves of balm were also used in poultices. An ointment or lotion made from elderflowers was used to soothe inflammation and speed the healing process, as were meadowsweet and flax. Eucalyptus was used in a compress to stop bleeding and accelerate healing.

Later, iodine was used on wounds, especially in wounds that had stopped bleeding.

woundwort

As the name suggests, woundwort was used in the healing of wounds. The bruised leaves were applied directly to the wounds to stop bleeding and accelerate the healing process.

Taken internally, it was used to treat internal bleeding and dysentery. It was also used to relieve gout, painful joints and cramp. Dizziness was also treated by it.

Y

yarrow

Yarrow is sometimes known as soldier's woundwort, milfoil and devil's nettle. Its botanical name is *Achillea millefolium*, so called because the Greek hero Achilles is supposed to have used it to treat the wounds of his warriors after battle.

In folklore, yarrow leaves were hung over the cradles of babies to keep away witches, and young women slept with it under their pillows so that they would dream of their future lovers.

It was used as an antiseptic in the treatment of wounds and to reduce inflammation and stop bleeding. Severe colds and fevers were treated with it since it induced perspiration. It was used in eruptive diseases such as measles and chickenpox to bring out the spots.

Yarrow was a popular aid to digestion, and kidney and liver disorders were also treated with it. High blood pressure was treated with it, and it was used to relieve varicose veins. It was used as a remedy for

yarrow

bleeding piles. As a diuretic it was used as a remedy for cystitis.

The herb was used as a tonic. If the head was washed with it, it was thought to improve baldness, stop hair from falling out and condition the hair. As a wash it was used to treat inflamed eyes.

Appendix

Some Old Remedies for Stains

blood stains
An old remedy for these suggested that a little starch was mixed and spread on the stains. This was washed off after a few hours.

coffee stains
One suggested remedy for these involved rubbing a little glycerine on the stain. The material was then washed in tepid water and ironed on the wrong side with a moderate iron until it was dry.

An alternative remedy involved making a 'soap' to wash the stain by mixing the yolk of an egg with a little water.

ink stains
Soaking something stained with ink in tinned tomato juice for about ten minutes and then washing it was an old suggested remedy.

Washing something stained with ink in warm milk

and then sprinkling the area of the stain with cornflour that was to be brushed off a day later was also recommended.

An old remedy for removing ink from linen involved melting a piece of tallow, dipping the stained part in it and then washing the linen.

Ink was said to be able to be removed from woollen materials by rubbing the stain with turpentine, having placed a pad beneath the area being rubbed.

iron-mould stains

One traditional remedy involved covering the stain with salt and then squeezing lemon juice over it. This was left for half an hour and then the material was washed in a weak solution of ammonia before being rinsed in clean water.

medicine stains

An old method of getting rid of medicine stains from silver spoons involved rubbing them with a piece of cloth dipped in dilute sulphuric acid and washing it off with soap suds.

Medicine stains on clothes were traditionally removed with fuller's earth or ammonia.

milk stains

According to an old remedy, the best way of getting rid

of milk stains from clothing was to soak the affected
area in a saucer of methylated spirits.

perspiration stains
A traditional way of removing perspiration stains from
garments involved placing the stained garment in warm
water containing a little ammonia. It was allowed to soak
for half an hour and then wrung out. If the stain was still
there, lemon juice was squeezed on it and the garment
rinsed in clean water and then washed.

wax stains
A traditional method of removing wax from material
was to place two thicknesses of blotting paper over the
stains and to press them with a moderately hot iron. As
the wax melted it was absorbed by the blotting paper.

wine stains
To remove these from linen tablecloths it was suggested
that the stained area was placed in some boiling milk
before being washed with soap and water. If the stain
was not completely removed, it was suggested that some
salt and a few drops of lemon juice be tried.

It was also suggested that salt was sprinkled over a
wine stain as soon as it occurred until further action could
be taken.